STAY TUNED

STAY TUNED

BEHIND THE SCREENS AT CHANNEL 5

PEGGY LAMSON

DAVID R. GODINE • *Publisher* • *Boston*

First published in 1988 by
David R. Godine, Publisher, Inc.
Horticultural Hall
300 Massachusetts Avenue
Boston, Massachusetts 02115

LIBRARY OF CONGRESS CATALOGING IN PUBLICATION DATA
Lamson, Peggy.
Stay tuned.
Includes index.
1. Television—Production and direction.
2. WCVB-TV (Television station : Boston, Mass.)
I. Title.
PN1992.75.L36   1988   791.45'023   86-46245
ISBN 0-87923-681-7

The two photographs in Chapter 2 are reproduced by
courtesy of Leo Beranek. All other photographs are
reproduced by courtesy of WCVB-TV; most were taken
by Steve Serio.

Designed by Dede Cummings

First edition

Printed in the United States of America

In
memory
of
Roy

CONTENTS

Sign-on   3

1. CORPORATE AMERICA STRIKES AGAIN   5

2. BBI: A LOOK BACKWARD   31

3. DAYTIME I: THE *EYEOPENER*,
5:30 TO 7:00 A.M.   57

4. DAYTIME II: *GOOD DAY!*, 10:00 TO 11:00 A.M., AND
MIDDAY NEWS, 12:00 TO 12:30 P.M.   74

5. ROLE MODELS   96

6. NEWSTIME: 6:00 TO 7:00 P.M.   117

7. PRIME ACCESS: *CHRONICLE*,
7:30 TO 8:00 P.M.   143

8. PRIME TIME: THREE SPECIALS,
8:00 TO 11:00 P.M.   167

9. WEEKEND   190

Sign-off   205

Index   226

STAY TUNED

Sign-on

WRITERS OF MYSTERY fiction sometimes say when they start a book, they don't know exactly how it will come out. Usually they have selected the victim since he or she must be put away early. But often they're not sure, until they get well into the book, and find out just who is to wield the knife, administer the poison, or shoot the gun with the silencer, or what the villain's motive will be.

Although this is clearly not a mystery story and is in fact not fiction at all, I still don't know, as I start to write, how it is going to come out. Nor do I know exactly who among many candidates will be the villain. I do, however, know the motive.

When I first had the idea for this book, it seemed quite straightforward. Too much print, I felt, had been devoted to glossy networks with their charismatic stars. And not enough had been written about local television, an integral link in our lives, providing the primary source of news for over 60 percent of the American people. Why not, then, write a book that would show the workings of a good local television station in a good market (televisionese for "city")?

And why not my own market, Boston, the sixth strongest in the country, and why not WCVB, Channel 5, widely regarded as one of the best stations—if not *the* best station—in America?

So I set to work to tell the story of how television works: the technology, the ratings, the sales, the programming, the "talent" (as the on-air personalities are called, usually to their disgust), the management, the sequence of owners, and finally—inevitably—the bottom line.

My goal was to write an objective book, a third-person account that would enlighten and, I hoped, entertain those who cared, and possibly even interest those who didn't know they cared.

I had started down this path with all the confidence I could muster—never very much confidence at the beginning of a project, as any writer knows— when all of a sudden, as we shall see, the path took a sharp unexpected turn and I found myself in muddied waters with a brand-new book.

So now I begin again, in the first person, with an ending I cannot foretell, to explore through the eyes of Channel 5, Boston, the world of local television today.

1

Corporate America Strikes Again

THE SIX P.M. NEWS AT
Channel 5, Boston, was just about seven minutes old and
nearing the end of the first segment when the story broke.
A bombshell.

As casually as if he were reading an everyday account of
a suburban school committee meeting, Chet Curtis, co-
anchor with his wife, Natalie Jacobson, read the words: "Metromedia Television is for sale."

He went on: "According to reports circulating widely on
Wall Street today, Metromedia, which owns and operates
seven television stations, *including this one*, will sell six of
these stations to Twentieth Century–Fox. The Hollywood-
based film and production company is half owned by Aus-
tralian publisher Rupert Murdoch.

"Channel 5, according to these and other reports, will not
be sold to Twentieth Century but to another group broadcaster. Unofficial sources indicate that this station will be
acquired by the Hearst Corporation. . . .

"There were no official comments from Robert Bennett, president of Metromedia Television and Radio, nor from John Kluge, principal owner of Metromedia, as to the reason for the sales.

"Obviously, as soon as we have more on this story we'll bring it to you."

Then, casually, as if they were merely reporting news rather than making it, Chet and Natalie "teased" the stories coming up in the next segment, and NewsCenter 5 went to commercial. The date: Thursday, May 2, 1985.

Hearing these ominous words coming out of the blue from my TV paralyzed me. But not for long. Almost before the commercial was over, I was out of the house, into my car, and heading south to the studio in Needham, Massachusetts, twenty minutes away.

Speeding along the turnpike, I tried to marshal my thoughts, at least to hastily put Channel 5's history into chronological order so that I would have some frame of reference for this most current event.

Twenty-three years earlier, in 1962, Channel 5 WCVB had been Channel 5 WHDH, which had for five years been run by the Boston *Herald Traveller* on a permit but without an official license from the Federal Communications Commission; it was considered by some, but by no means all, to be a humdrum, mediocre station.

After a bitter ten-year struggle, the FCC finally took the permit away from WHDH, primarily on the grounds of media diversification, which mandated against one company owning a newspaper and a television station in the same market. The license was awarded to Boston Broadcasters, Inc. (BBI). This group of distinguished, visionary Boston citizens was committed to the cause not only of local ownership but of local participation in management. Among other pledges, all of which were honored, BBI promised the FCC an unprecedented fifty hours a week of local programming.

To help implement these and other seemingly impossible obligations to the regulatory agency, BBI hired Robert Bennett away from Metromedia, Inc. to be the station manager. Bennett was said to be one of the best local broadcasters in the country.

Along with his enlightened board of directors, Bennett set a new standard for excellent, innovative local broadcasting that was to have a stimulating influence on the entire industry.

Ten years later, however, dedication aside and money to the fore, BBI decided to sell its brainchild to Metromedia for an unprecedented sum of $220 million. They chose Metromedia, a corporation not known for its interest in local broadcasting, because Bob Bennett, who was subsequently to return to Metromedia, had remained close to the legendary John Kluge, president and 73 percent owner of the company.

Accordingly WCVB-Metromedia went on the air as such in May 1982 with noble pledges made by Kluge, Bennett, and other corporate titans in the company, that *quality broadcasting* was and would continue to be Metromedia's primary, overriding aim, especially for this station, which they considered the jewel in their crown studded with stations in Boston, Houston, New York, Washington, Los Angeles, Dallas, and Chicago.

And now, in May 1985, three years later, Metromedia was selling all seven of its stations to Rupert Murdoch for—as I was soon to find out—$2 billion. Murdoch in turn would spin off Boston's Channel 5 to the Hearst Corporation for $450 million, the highest price ever paid for a local television station.*

Furthermore it seemed a time of open season on media

*Two weeks later this figure was eclipsed, however, when the Tribune Company acquired station KTLA-TV, Los Angeles, for $510 million.

The Newsroom

takeovers, with ABC being acquired by Capital Cities and buccaneer Ted Turner making a strong bid for a hostile takeover of CBS, to mention only the two most prominent ones of that month. There would be others, all threatening the very concept of local ownership.

Inside the station I headed at once for its nerve center, the Newsroom. The building that houses WCVB was once a Caterpiller tractor repair factory, and the part that is now the Newsroom must have been a huge storage space with enough height to raise a sixty-foot crane. Ceilings have since been lowered, raised again, then relowered to provide a second story with offices, which are reached by a spiral staircase.

The result is a forty- by seventy-foot area, sprawling yet

intimate, chaotic yet effective. It looks like backstage at the Shubert Theatre, or perhaps more likely at an arena theater—The Circle in the Square—with the set (studio) raised at one end of the room and the glassed-in control room seen behind it.

In the large, red-carpeted, windowless room are three large cloverleaf tables, called pods. Each has five seats; each belongs to a separate news program.

As I arrive, the six o'clock news has just finished, and overhead lights are being turned off; Chet Curtis and Natalie Jacobson are just stepping down from the platform. The place is jammed: every seat at every pod is taken— not an unusual circumstance at this hour, but the hushed, strained atmosphere is noticeably different. Many of the staff have learned of the sale either just before air time or when they first heard the words coming from Chet's mouth.

Chet and Natalie† are surrounded and are assuming a properly encouraging leadership role. "We got through a sale three years ago," says Natalie. "No reason why we can't do it again."

My entrance is greeted with variations on the theme of "Well, you've sure got a new book now, haven't you?"

I head immediately for Chet—the friendliest, most approachable of men, always good for the latest word as befits the experienced news reporter that he is. "What's it all about?"

"I didn't know myself until about a half-hour ago," he says. Linda Polach, producer of the six o'clock news, who has been at her post in the control room during the show, joins the group, pronouncing herself in a state of shock, and says that she, who has to format, time, and supervise the entire show,

---

†I have chosen to use the given names of the on-air personalities because that is the way they refer to each other on air at all TV stations: "Back to you, Chet,"— or Jack, or Tom or Liz.

Natalie Jacobson   Chet Curtis

didn't know either until she was given a hundred and fifty
words of copy and told to find a space for it somewhere in
the first segment.

There had of course been rumblings the day before when
the *Wall Street Journal* reported that "sources" indicated
that Fox Films and Metromedia were discussing "some sort
of combination." The next day, May 2, the morning before
the news broke on the air, the *New York Times* picked up
the story, stating that Murdoch was engaged in "serious"
negotiations to acquire some of the television stations owned
by Metromedia. The *Wall Street Journal*'s follow-up story
added for the first time the news that Metromedia intended
to sell the Boston station, "widely considered the jewel
among its broadcast properties," separately and was thought
to be asking about $400 million for it.

Neither story was prominently played, nor was there any

mention in either as to who might ultimately be the pur-
chaser of WCVB-Boston.

Such was the state of affairs when Chet and Natalie arrived
for work a little after three on that fateful Thursday afternoon.
Rumors abounding, facts in scarce supply, tension and frustration in the Newsroom mounting, people felt like displaced
orphans, waiting to see which foster parent was going to pick
them up this time.

"It was driving me crazy," Chet said. "Not knowing." Not
knowing why WCVB was being specially treated in the
seven-station sale (if indeed there really was going to *be* a
sale), although thanking their stars they were apparently not
going to become Rupert Murdoch's property. Not knowing
what role Bob Bennett, their guardian angel, worshiped by
most staffers at WCVB, was playing in all this.

"My fantasy," said Chet, "is that Bob is the one who has
spared us Murdoch as his final gesture to this station that
he loved so much."

Finally someone—no one seems to remember just who—
threw down the gauntlet to Chet Curtis. "You're the best
reporter. For God's sake find out somehow who is going to
own us."

Chet, needing no urging, seized the phone and went to
work. Shortly before five, he ran one of the copy packs (six
different-colored sheets separated by carbons) into his typewriter and, in the huge print used for all on-air copy, wrote
a single word and handed it to Natalie.

I have the page in my file right now. The word is
Rosebud. Natalie understood at once: Rosebud equals
Hearst. (In Orson Wells's famous movie *Citizen Kane*, about
William Randolph Hearst, Rosebud was the name of a little
old-fashioned sled, the kind with high, round front runners,
that the young Hearst character had cherished as a small
boy. It plays a significant symbolic role throughout *Citizen*

Philip Scribner Balboni, Vice President/News

Kane. Readers may even remember that the last shot of the film is of the little sled burning in a furnace with just the faded word *Rosebud* visible.)

By then they were edging up to air time. Chet and Natalie ran up the spiral staircase to the office of Phil Balboni, vice-president in charge of news and confronted him with Rosebud.

Balboni, looking haggard and distraught for reasons they would soon discover, told them that during the day Bob Bennett had finally confirmed that a sale had been consummated and would be announced over the weekend. He and other top management were being requested to go to New York the following day to meet with the new owners—still unnamed. But speculation was increasing that it was indeed Hearst. And now Balboni agreed with his anchor team that they would have to take some note of the situation on their evening news. So, clinging as always to the "unofficial sources" he himself wrote the words that Chet Curtis read.

I noticed a lot of movement in the Newsroom as people headed up the spiral stairs.

"What's going on?" I asked Natalie Jacobson.

"Phil Balboni has called a meeting in his office for the whole news staff."

Although I had often sat in on staff meetings at WCVB, I still had misgivings about injecting myself into this one, which seemed such a family affair. Yet I knew I had to try, so I followed the others up the stairs.

Phil Balboni was sitting on the edge of his desk looking more devastated than I had ever seen him. "Phil," I asked, "may I please sit in?"

He stared at me for the longest time. The room quieted down and waited. Finally, in a barely audible voice, he said, "I'd rather you didn't." I nodded and fled.

When I got downstairs, Paul La Camera, vice-president in charge of programming, was just walking through the Newsroom. He and Balboni and general manager S. James Coppersmith are the three top executives. They make an interesting contrast: Balboni, brilliant, intense, a windmill tilter; La Camera, idealistic, intellectual, laid back; and Coppersmith, aggressive, sharp, witty, and gutsy.

Paul La Camera, after the usual reference to the new book I now had, pronounced "It will be better," then added almost casually, "even though we five didn't get the station."

Even though we five didn't get the station! I stared at him trying not to look blank, having learned in this business always to act as if you knew what people were talking about and then try to find out later.

But on this occasion, since I apparently failed to look even faintly convincing, La Camera explained. "You knew that the five of us, Phil Balboni, me, Jim Coppersmith, and two others, have been negotiating for weeks to buy the station and to have it owned by the employees."

I was staggered and distressed. What a happy ending *that* would have made. But $450 million! It was almost obscene. "Where on earth could you possibly have gotten that unheard-of kind of money?"

He laughed. "Kidder Peabody, with whom we have been dealing, had assured us that it was doable. Not easy, God knows, but doable." He looked at his watch. "I've got to run to *Chronicle* now" (the station's super 7:30-to-8:00 magazine-format program). "But that's what Phil is telling the staff right now. How close we came and then at the last minute failed." He hurried out, calling over this shoulder, "Good for you for getting right out here" without telling me *why* they had failed.

And in truth I still find that "why" a somewhat gray area, although I have been told the facts over and over. It seems that the legendary Metromedia president, John Kluge, who knew of the aspirations of the five executives as spearheaded by Phil Balboni and who did nothing to discourage them in the belief that their chances were good, at the last minute uncorked a "prior commitment" to the Hearst Company, which he claimed he felt bound to honor.

In a relatively short time the news staff all trooped down from the meeting in Phil Balboni's office, looking, I thought, cheerful enough, considering. "You didn't miss much," Chet Curtis reported. "It was all rather emotional and of course very sad that the local group couldn't get the station, but Phil had good things to say about Hearst, and we were all assured we were going to keep our jobs."

"The only thing to worry about," Natalie Jacobson added, "is if they fire either Jim Coppersmith or Phil Balboni. But if those guys stay on, it will be just the same."

"Sure it will," said Chet, sounding only faintly like whistling in the dark. But then, warming to his theme: "After all, I was working for the old *Herald Traveller* station when BBI took it over, and we all thought, 'Oh, they don't know anything about television. What are they going to do?' Then we all loved BBI. Then BBI sold to Metromedia and we all said, 'That's a lousy, mediocre outfit, and it won't be any good at all,' and actually Metromedia built us a great new studio and made the station much better. So therefore we've got to take an upbeat view now."

Hear, hear! Sort of.

As I left the building a few minutes later I ran into Balboni, also leaving. He too seemed relatively cheerful. "We can't miss, you know," he said. "We've twice been the biggest money-making station in the business, so ask yourself, as we have, why would Hearst want to change anything in a station that's making this much money?"

I could think of a few reasons, such as to make more money, such as the old-fashioned perception of Hearst and yellow journalism being synonymous, such as Hearst's early reputation in television as unimaginative, such as, more specifically, Hearst acquiring the punch-drunk *Herald Traveller* after it lost the TV station and just about delivering the *coup de grace* to that dying organization until it was rescued— ironically—by Rupert Murdoch (if you like that kind of rescue).

Still, even that evening I had heard several positive references to a different spirit in the Hearst Corporation, much changed in the past six years under the leadership of a strong chief executive officer named Frank Bennack.

As Balboni turned to go he promised that just as soon as he could he would give me the entire story of his and his colleagues' attempts to acquire WCVB. "And it will be soon," he said.

I said good night to Phil Balboni and wished him the good sleep he looked as if he needed.

Three weeks later Balboni made good on his promise. In the meantime, after a flurry of front-page stories in the *Boston Globe* (Murdoch's *Boston Herald* ignored the entire affair), after one indignant Op-Ed piece calling the FCC to account for its high-handed practice, one blast in a weekly underground paper against conglomerates and speculators stealing the public airways, and one inconclusive press conference attended by Bob Bennett and Frank Bennack of the Hearst Corporation, the excitement had pretty well quieted down.

Jim Coppersmith had told his staff at their first weekly meeting after the sale was consummated, "We'll be feeling in a state of limbo. There will be a tendency on the part of the corporation that is selling us to ignore us, and on the part of the corporation that is buying us to be temporarily handcuffed. All this can have a devastating effect. But I won't allow that to happen. I want the same sense of excitement to continue here as usual. We have to act as if we own this station, and I urge you to keep that thought in mind."

It must have been an exceedingly difficult thought for Balboni to keep in mind—to *act* as if he owned what he and his cohorts had thought they had a very good chance of actually owning.

"You know, our effort to acquire this station and keep it in local hands goes back quite a ways," he told me when we had our meeting. "We're talking 1980–81 now, when pressures were building within the Board of BBI to sell the station."

"Was there any possible reason they wanted to sell except for money?"

"No, there couldn't have been any other reason, although you'll find a certain amount of revisionist history going on among some of the directors these days. It's hard to find anybody who actually says they wanted to sell, but the fact is that the majority *did* want to. And when I became aware of their positive intent to sell, I talked to Tim Johnson [the doctor who was first introduced on television in the early BBI days in a program called *House Call* and who is now with ABC although still stationed in Boston] and Paul La Camera about our making an attempt. Our interest was genuine, but it didn't have any heft or any real credibility. We were never taken seriously as an alternative, so when Bob Bennett engineered the sale to Kluge at Metromedia in July '81 and consummated it in May '82, we were just helpless bystanders. BBI bailed out and left us behind to pick up the pieces."

I told Balboni of my compulsion as a reporter to assign the blame for what was now happening somewhere—to some villains. Had I found possible candidates here among this so-much-admired group of Boston citizens?

Phil Balboni thought in a way I had. "In that first sale to Metromedia," he said, "we were damaged internally. We lost momentum, we lost stature in the eyes of the press and the public. I don't think I ever worked harder than in those first eighteen months that Metromedia owned us to hold this station on track, to fight for what we believed in, and to keep the place motivated. And that's something those people who sold out will never appreciate and probably don't care about. And as far as I'm concerned, if I live a thousand years I'll never forgive them for it."

On that bitter note, we moved to contemplate the current and third change of ownership.

It seemed that a few months earlier Balboni had had a hunch that a sale of WCVB might be in the offing. His suspicion was based partly on the growing laxity of the FCC

Paul La Camera

concerning the number of stations a corporation could own, and partly on the fiscal situation at Metromedia. A year ago John Kluge had taken his company private, meaning that he bought it back from the stockholders, saddling the company with $1.3 billion of debt. Wall Street calls this a leveraged buy-out. It was financed in this case by junk bonds, so called because of the low credit rating of the issuer. With all this red ink staring Kluge in the face, selling off one of his properties was not an outlandish possibility.

With this thought in mind, Balboni along with Johnson and La Camera arranged a meeting with Bob Bennett, who was by then president of Metromedia Television and Radio. Bennett had tried for a while to make Boston Metromedia's corporate headquarters, building fancy new offices at the Needham station. In so doing he expected to keep a weather eye on his godchild, station WCVB. However, given his hope of transforming Metromedia into something akin to a fourth network, the pull of the West Coast was too strong. He was moving his operation to California on February 15, the day before he met with Balboni and the other two men.

"We were all good friends of Bob's, so it was a very cordial discussion," said Balboni. "He was respectful of our interest, but said that he had no idea whether the station would be sold. 'It certainly is not for sale right now,' he said, 'but if I were ever to find out that there was such a possibility, I promise I'd let you know.'

"He also said such things as 'where would you get the money?' and we said we didn't really know just then, but we had reason to believe we could put together a credible effort, and in any event we wanted to try. We'd lived through this once before, and we didn't want to see the chance pass us by again."

Some weeks later, on April 4, according to Balboni's calendar, Bob Bennett was back in Boston. At the station, following the six o'clock news, he took Balboni to one side of the Newsroom to say, "I just want to tell you I think something may be happening." He had no definite knowledge, but he felt that in the current takeover atmosphere, the forces at work in the industry were getting to his boss, John Kluge. He himself had been told absolutely nothing and most likely would not be until whatever was going to happen was a *fait accompli*. Kluge, he said, liked to play his cards very close to his chest and make his own deals. Still Bennett felt that something was afoot, and he was dismayed to think it might be a sale of WCVB.

Phil Balboni was galvanized into action. "I'm now going into high gear," he told Bennett.

Balboni, La Camera, and Johnson, the three conspirators—for that is how they had begun to think of their role in this clandestine effort—met the next morning to plan their strategy.

They decided first to expand the group to include Tom Bringola, business manager of the station, who they knew had a bit more sophisticated money sense than any of them. They also felt that Jim Coppersmith's participation as general manager would be very important for their cause, and promptly went to his office to ask if he wanted to join them. He did.

Five days later, prepared to wrestle with the hard, cold-cash reality of their dream, Balboni and Bringola went to New York to talk with the firm of Kidder Peabody about the financial viability of their plans. Although all five men were well paid, none was really rich, and the sum involved—a sum they could only guess at since they were not privy to Metromedia's books—was enormous. In fact, they guessed it right on the nose—$450 million.

Kidder Peabody is said to have special expertise in both debt funding (bank loans) and equity funding (individuals or groups who have a great deal of money to invest and look for a high return on a business that is already a going concern with a proven track record). Channel 5, according to Kidder Peabody, readily qualified for both kinds of financing.

Strongly in its favor was that the station had in three short years appreciated in resale value from $220 million to $450 million. At this rate of growth the annual net profit (the actual figure is a closely guarded secret, but $35 million is a safe bet) would in five years be $45 million to $50 million.

All this added up to good news for the five executives. In a word that came to be used practically hourly, it was "doable."

The next hurdle was to ask Bennett if he could arrange a meeting with John Kluge so the five could present their case. This was potentially the most difficult challenge so far; Balboni said they were afraid their request would be turned down flat either because the station had already been sold or because Kluge would consider their offer presumptuous. Neither of these misgivings was unjustified in view of the man they were hoping to deal with.

A seventy-year-old tycoon, Kluge had come to this country as a German immigrant at age eight. He is looked upon as polite, secretive, sly, and effective—not surprisingly, since the name Kluge (the final *e* is pronounced) means "clever" in German.

In 1959 he bought a small broadcasting company, which he promptly built into a $50-million-a-year firm. In addition he owns an outdoor billboard company, the Harlem Globe Trotters, and the Ice Capades. More recently his primary interest has been in telecommunications, which in his case means paging systems and, more important, cellular telephones, considered the wave of the future in bringing car-driving executives closer to their home offices. His reputation is of a man who cares little about the details of whatever enterprise he is involved in so long as he is making money. This he does in great abundance; he is one of the world's few billionaires. He never gives interviews.

When word came through Bob Bennett that yes, Mr. Kluge would be delighted to see them, Balboni and company could not help feeling elated. Surely this was the sign they had been waiting for.

The meeting took place on April 24, 1985, in the offices of Metromedia's New York City radio station, WNEW. "We had planned our presentation carefully," said Balboni. "Jim Coppersmith spoke first and made a kind of general introductory remark. I followed with a brief discussion of the financial aspect, and Tim Johnson wound up on a rather personal note."

Through all this Kluge listened attentively. Then he said, "You gentlemen know that I always keep my word, and you know that I've always lived by that rule. So I must now tell you that I did give my word to someone else that if the station was ever sold, they would have the opportunity to buy it."

Now, no one—not one of the five potential buyers, to each of whom I asked the question—could fathom why, this being the case, Kluge had ever agreed to see them—his own people—without first warning them of his prior commitment.

It was true, he did go on to say, that there was always a possibility that the person to whom he had made the commitment might not, for a variety of technical reasons, wish to exercise his option to buy the station. He told them "If for some reason the deal does not go through, I give you my word that you will be the next people I will come to."

Cold comfort indeed, although Phil Balboni says he tried to keep his spirits up by clinging to that thin thread. Not so Jim Coppersmith, who believes himself, with some justification, to be the most objective of the group and who doesn't think they ever really had a chance. "I think," he told me, "that Big does not sell to Little. Big *buys* Little and otherwise only does business with Big."

"Which in this case means the Hearst Company?" Coppersmith nodded. "But can you tell me why their $450 million in cash was any different from your $450 million in cash?"

"Because I think instinctively Kluge knows that five years from now he might want to buy the station back, or buy three Hearst newspapers, or sell them something else—the Harlem Globe Trotters or Foster & Klaiser outdoor advertising. If he sells us this TV station, even though he knows it might be better for the community, he knows he's never going to sell us anything else."

"In other words, there's no idealism at all?"

"Idealism in the boardrooms of major corporations?" Coppersmith snorted. "I've never seen it."

But Phil Balboni, the instigator, could not reconcile himself to this bitter realism.

"I had a very strong sense of destiny about this particular time," he told me as we sat together in his office reviewing the whole sorry story. "We had the people who had all the experience and expertise. We were in the right position to control this station and to return to the community and to the employees what they each deserved. We could have raised the money and kept the dream of local ownership alive. And to have that opportunity snatched away from us is a bitter, profound, lifetime disappointment.

"And I don't mind saying as I sit here right now that I don't think enough was done to ensure that this station would have stayed in local hands. I don't blame the Hearst Corporation one bit. I lay the blame squarely at the door of John Kluge and, sadly, I'm afraid I also have to lay it at the door of my good friend Bob Bennett."

Here, of course, is the real mystery figure—hero or erstwhile hero, Robert M. Bennett. Had he betrayed the station he had created and then in 1981 helped to sell to alien if not hostile hands? Had he been aware of the Hearst connection when he first talked to Phil Balboni about his suspicion that something was afoot? Was he aware of it at the time of the WNEW meeting with Kluge? And did he try to do anything to derail the Hearst deal, as Kluge had hinted might be possible, in the hope of getting the station back not only into local hands but into the hands of five men he knew, had worked with, loved, and trusted?

After what seemed a frustratingly long period of conjecture, I finally had an opportunity to question Bob Bennett himself, somewhat along the lines of Senator Howard Baker during the Watergate hearings, "What did you know and when did you know it?"

At the press conference held three days after the sales to Murdoch and Hearst were announced, Bob Bennett was asked if he felt sad at the way things had turned out. He had, after all, been president of Metromedia Television, and now with all seven stations sold out from under him, he had nothing left to be president of.

"If I had my druthers," Bennett answered, "I'd rather this hadn't happened. When I look back on the sale of the stations it's like the end of a little Camelot."

"But are you sad?" the questioner persisted.

"Yes," said Bennett with finality. "I'm sad and depressed."

Bennett having made an estimated $20 million from the sale of the Metromedia stations, this answer called forth a number of under-the-breath comments, variations on the "crying all the way to the bank" theme.

But perhaps this was unfair. He had already garnered quite a few million dollars (five is the estimate) from the sale of WCVB to Metromedia, so in fact what he had cared about, when everything appeared to be going so rosily for him, was not more cash, which he didn't need, but the opportunity to create a fourth network of independent stations. He came close to this goal, he believed, only to stumble at the five-yard line.

Later Bennett described his feelings to me privately in a little allegory, one that he had regaled John Kluge with when Kluge told him he had sold the television stations. It is a very Bennettesque recitation.

"I told him it felt a little bit like it was 1895 and he said to me, 'Hey, come on, Bob, we're going in the stagecoach business, you and the other three guys in the office of the president.' And I said, 'Okay, what are we going to do?' And he said, 'We're going to see who can get from New York to Los Angeles first, and *you're* going to sit in the stagecoach and *you're* going to hold the reins.'

"So I said, 'Right, let's go.' And we tear along through rivers and streams and plains and the dust is flying and I'm holding onto the reins like a son of a bitch, and I say, 'I don't know if we're out in front, but I think we are.' And then one night we get to Albuquerque and put up in a little dump of a hotel. And I come down in the morning, and the guys are taking the horses *off* the coach instead of putting them on. And I say, 'What are you doing?' And Kluge says, 'Bob, I don't know how to tell you this, but we sold the stagecoach last night.' And I say, '*You sold the stagecoach?*' And he says, 'Yeah, we did. We're out of business.' And then they're putting saddles on the horses, and Kluge comes over to me and starts stuffing my pockets with gold. And I say, 'What are you doing that for?' And he says, 'That's your share. See ya.' And with that, he and the others ride off.

"So I've got three things I can do. I can either put a saddle on the remaining horse and ride off in some direction, or I can attach the horse to the stagecoach, but I don't think one horse can pull it alone, or I can turn around and buy the hotel we slept in last night. And not one of those three scenarios is one I want, or one I have written for myself."

When I went in July for my meeting with Bennett at his Cape Cod condominium, the meeting at which this discourse took place, my attitude toward this demigod, whom I had met briefly only once, was exceedingly wary. All the glowing reports from people at WCVB and elsewhere had emphasized his charm, his warmth, his vast energy, his friendliness, his wit, his superb abilities as a salesman. "He has a sense of both excitement and vulnerability about him," says Jim Coppersmith. "It's an experience to meet him. When you talk to him, he has the facility of convincing you that you're the most important person in the world to him."

Well, I wasn't going to be taken in—not by any of the charisma, not by his huge, powerful frame, his superengaging smile, his ease of manner, nor even by the fact that, being on vacation, he was growing a stubby little beard that made him look rather like Captain Kidd.

No, I was *not* going to be disarmed by him. But in the event, of course, I was—almost. Just a few little comments of his gave me pause.

There came a time when I had to ask him point-blank if he had been aware of Kluge's so-called commitment to sell Channel 5 to Hearst.

"I didn't know about that," he said.

"I can't believe," I told him, "that with your intimate connection with WCVB for all those years, you wouldn't have known anything about your boss's plans for its future."

"I didn't have any idea," he said. "First of all, earlier, when there was talk of selling CVB, to reduce Metromedia's debt I talked Kluge out of it. I said, 'John, you can't do that to this town again. They've been through the whole history of WHDH, BBI, and Metromedia. It would be a disaster for them. Sell New York, sell Los Angeles, but not Boston.' "

And as he spoke it crossed my mind fleetingly: if Kluge was talking of selling Boston, would he not have been likely to tell Bennett that he had a ready buyer in Hearst, to whom he had already committed the station?

"So," Bennett repeated, "I talked him out of it. He said to me, 'Okay, we won't do it.' And then he went ahead on his own and did it. He not only sold Boston, he sold the whole damn thing—including the television company of which I was president. And before I even knew it was happening. I was devastated. I mean absolutely devastated."

I asked him then if, inasmuch as Boston was going to be sold separately, there wasn't something he could have done to persuade Kluge to sell the station to Phil Balboni and his colleagues.

"I was pulling for them," he said. "I wanted them to have it. I talked to Kluge for them. But in my heart of hearts I don't think it could have worked."

"You're not saying you don't think they could have run the station satisfactorily, are you?"

"No, of course not. There's no question that they could have run it probably even better than they will now working for somebody else."

(Unspoken query: is the public interest thus being better served by having them working for somebody else?)

"What I'm saying," Bennett went on, "is that $450 million is an awful lot of money and to service that debt at at least ten percent—probably it would have been more—would mean $45 to $50 million in interest alone."

But, as I pointed out, they never envisaged owing $450 million. The equity partner was going to own $150 million, so they were always talking in terms of interest on $300 million.

"Well, even at $300 million, paying probably fifteen percent, you're talking about $45 million interest, and the station only makes $35 million [state secret out of the bag here], so they've got to be in the hole $10 million just to pay the interest."

"But the station's revenue is projected to appreciate up to $50 million a year by 1990," I said, reflecting that he himself had told me earlier that when the station was sold to Metromedia in 1981 the annual profit was $20 million and that three years later the profit was $35 million. "So we went up $15 million in three years," he had said.

And I had replied that it seemed a television company couldn't fail to make money these days. "It's pretty difficult," Bennett had answered. "You've got to be pretty dumb not to make it work."

Still, in fairness, there is no denying that $450 million *is* a lot of money even if you only have to pay interest on $300 million of it. Phil Balboni and the other four all realized that there was going to have to be considerable belt-tightening at Channel 5 for the rest of the decade to service their debt.

Bennett thought it would have been more than simple belt-tightening. "I think they would have been forced to do the very thing that would have killed them if Metromedia or Hearst had done it. They would have had to cut back on staff, cut back on program ideas, cut back on *Chronicle*. Oh, don't get me wrong," he added, I thought a touch defensively. "I was pulling for them because I loved them, and I knew how badly they wanted it. I wanted them to have it, but at the same time I think God was looking down on them because I don't think they could have made it."

"Did you tell them that?"

"I said to Phil and to all four of those other guys, 'Don't get so emotional that you're irrational.'

"Hearst thought it was grossly overpriced, too," he went on. "But I convinced them. I actually sold the idea of buying the station to Hearst." (Passing thought. If Hearst had rejected Kluge's offer, Balboni and company had been promised the next chance.) "After all"—Bennett laughed—"CVB is my kid. I had to make goddamn sure it was going to somebody that would take care of it."

In sum, Bennett's role in supporting the sale to the five executives can, I believe, best be summed up as *pro forma*. He had done what he had been asked to do by Phil Balboni and the others, first tipping them off to a possible sale in the offing, then, while not actually discouraging their aspirations, urging them to think rationally, and finally arranging for them to meet with Kluge to present their case.

Since he says emphatically that he did not know of the commitment to Hearst before the fact, one must believe him.

On the other hand, it seems perfectly clear that he made no real effort to prevent or even to stall the Hearst sale so that the Balboni group could, as promised by Kluge, have a crack at it. On the contrary, by his own admission, he actually *persuaded* Frank Bennack at Hearst to buy the station. He even had another chance to call them off when the Hearst people, before they would make a deal, asked him for a "noncompete" contract, which meant that he would agree not to go to work for any competing stations in the Boston market. Had he refused to sign such an agreement, as he did when the Murdoch people asked for the same thing for the other six stations ("Screw you," he told them succinctly), Hearst probably would not have signed, and Balboni and company again would have had their chance.

That he did not extend himself further on behalf of his friends at WCVB is explainable in terms of his apparently honestly held belief that the financial stakes were too high for them and would have actually crippled their ability to run WCVB.

Against this view of his, however, one must weigh the

S. James Coppersmith, Vice President/General Manager

position of Balboni, La Camera, Johnson, Bringola, and Coppersmith. These five men singly and certainly collectively are every bit as savvy as Bennett about the financial realities of their station and of the media in general. They would never in the world have undertaken to buy Channel 5 if they had thought they might have been forced by the money pinch to decimate the station that they cared so deeply about.

They believed implicitly, bolstered in their conviction by Kidder Peabody, that they would succeed. They understood that they would have to cut out frills, freeze salaries, eschew new, expensive program ideas, and generally settle for the status quo for a period of at least five years. After that, they would have been golden.

"In five years," says Jim Coppersmith, "the equity would have appreciated so that the cash flow would have improved, which means ultimately we could have had a TV station that no one in the country has ever envisaged. It would have been a place where the employees were owners, where profits were not a primary consideration, where we could have become an institution in the life of this community in the same sense that Harvard and MIT are. And besides that, we would have had a hell of a lot of fun running this kind of station."

So who has won? Kluge, that's who. Bennett is out of a job and the five WCVB executives are out of a dream, but Kluge has his "stack," as Bennett calls it. "Kluge measures how well he's done in life by the size of his stack," he explains. He wanted to be a billionaire and now he is. There're only maybe fifteen of those in the whole world, so now he can say only fifteen guys are as smart as I am and have built their stacks as high as me."

And what of the Federal Communications Commission, theoretically constituted to uphold the integrity of licenses to broadcast, which are granted in the public's name and for which the licensees pay nothing? Did they make any move to assure or even investigate whether the public interest was being served by this sale? They did not.

All of which leaves us to wonder if the television industry can any longer be looked on as a public trust. Or is it now only a vast moneymaking business?

Stay tuned.

2

BBI: A Look Backward

W<small>HEN</small> BBI <small>SIGNED ON</small>
the air for the first time at 3:00 A.M. on March 19, 1972,
their jubilant opening words, "Hello, world!," culminated
ten long years of frustration, dashed hopes, setbacks, let-
downs, foul-ups, and monkey wrenches thrown into the
gears.

Their objective during this interminable period had been
to take away from WHDH the authority to operate VHF
station Channel 5 in Boston. In fact this authority, amounting
only to a *de facto* license, was granted in 1957 by a weak,
careless, FCC that in the eyes of many who followed the
case should never have awarded it in the first place. Among
its other shortcomings, the station's blatant lack of media
diversification amounted to a violation of the Sherman An-
titrust Act.

WHDH-TV, owned and operated by the Boston *Herald
Traveller* Corporation, had what has been called a "com-

munications stronghold" in Boston,* owning one newspaper (a Republican newspaper, incidentally, during the Republican administration of President Eisenhower), one FM station, and one AM station. Clearly this gave them an unfair competitive advantage over Boston's other newspaper, the *Globe*, especially since commercial time on WHDH was habitually sold in conjunction with space in the *Herald* and *Traveller* newspapers, to say nothing of the constant identification of news on the air as *Herald* or *Traveller* news, and other sly reciprocal advantages.

The Boston case, as it came to be known in regulatory circles in Washington, raised some eyebrows in the Legislative Oversight Committee. But not enough eyebrows to change the status quo of WHDH.

It was not until President Kennedy appointed a brilliant young Chicago lawyer, Newton Minow, as chairman of the FCC that a new broom began sweeping various piles of dirt from under various rugs. However, despite the strong disapproval of the new chairman, the FCC, probably hoping to get rid of the whole tiresome case on the grounds that possession was nine-tenths of the law, granted WHDH a four months' license to operate—the first official recognition that the station had had in five years.

Minow's response to this action was to state that new applicants were invited to file applications in competition with WGBH in what was called a comprehensive hearing.

Enter BBI, with its stellar list of stockholders, its historians, physicists, biologists, anthropologists, economists, engineers, doctors, judges, and captains of industry—along with two other applicants, one perennial, Greater Boston II, and the other—Charles River—new.

*I am indebted for material about the WHDH-FCC contretempts to Sterling Red Quinlan's book, *The Hundred Million Dollar Lunch* (Chicago: J. Philip O'Hara, 1974).

There followed an endless hearing, lasting just under two years, conducted by a thoughtful, scholarly, and essentially fair-minded lawyer named Herbert Sharfman. After listening to BBI's proposal of (1) twenty-four hours of broadcasting, seven days a week, (2) fifty hours weekly of live local programming (the most anyone had heard of in those days was twenty-three hours), (3) one-quarter of its ownership to be sold to employees for ten dollars a share, (4) profits always held secondary to quality, (5) fewer commercials than allowable under National Association of Broadcasters guidelines, (6) extremely high integration of ownership into the station's daily operation, Sharfman observed dryly that he found the BBI proposals "permeated by an exuberance which makes one doubtful of their fulfillment."

He ended by finding in favor of WHDH, granting them a license for three years, subject, of course, to the approval of the seven FCC commissioners.

Still BBI refused to give up and opted, along with the other three applicants (WHDH included), to go for the long shot of an oral argument before the FCC itself. Newton Minow had gone on to greener fields by then, and two of the commissioners had disqualified themselves, allegedly because of conflict of interest but perhaps because of plain weariness. Another was to back out just before the hearings began.

Miraculously, however, the four remaining commissioners voted three to one in favor of BBI. It was almost not to be believed. The saying in broadcast circles had always been that "the Commission giveth but doth not take away."

It then took sixteen more months for the commissioners to commit their decision to writing and to state that in their judgment "the grant of the application to BBI would best serve the public interest." One might think that was the end of it, but actually there were to be four more years of litigation, during which the *Herald Traveller* showed a stupendous variety of bared fangs. From the outset it was clear they weren't going to take the FCC decision, especially since it reversed that of the hearing examiner, Sharfman, in their favor, without mounting a vigorous counterattack.

And in truth most of the broadcast industry was on their side (in many cases, of course, fearing the same fate for themselves), offering tenders of support to Harold Clancy, chief executive officer of the Herald Traveller Corporation.

When WHDH's petition to the FCC for a reconsideration was turned down, they took their case to the Court of Appeals (Nixon was by then president), which, after a comparatively short delay of five months, *upheld* the FCC decision in favor of BBI. As a matter of course WHDH then asked for another reconsideration, and when this was turned down, the case moved on the last leg of its first journey (there would be three) to the U.S. Supreme Court.

Meanwhile, a WHDH goon squad inspired by Harold Clancy launched a no-holds-barred campaign against every member of the board of BBI, branding each director they could with the slightest and most trivial of peccadilloes, each case being overblown and prominently played on the front pages of the *Herald Traveller*.

I should in fairness point out that there was a great deal at stake for the *Herald Traveller*. If they lost WHDH, they knew the newspaper would doubtless go under too, costing some two thousand jobs and leaving Boston with one only major newspaper, the *Globe* (Democratic) and one tabloid, the *Record American*.

But for the time being at least their desperation tactics were not paying off. On June 14, 1971, the Supreme Court turned down WHDH's appeal for a review of the case. Victory for BBI, and what they had every reason to believe would be a mid-September start-up, was now in sight.

However, the actual document assuring them of this did not come into BBI's hands until the end of June. Then there

First signal ever on air: During a waiting period BBI was
allowed a brief test each night—this was September 11, 1971,
5:00 A.M., Leo Beranek and son Tom

was *another* month's delay while they waited for the FCC
to issue a construction permit. Meanwhile they had bought
the Caterpillar repair factory in Needham and arranged to
lease from Channel 4, the Westinghouse station, space on
its existing antenna, also in Needham. At the base of this
tower they had to construct a transmitter building.

Here I turn the mike over to Leo Beranek, noted acoustical
engineer, and the man chosen by the board to devote full
time to BBI as its president.

"How do you take a building," he asks rhetorically, "and
change it from nothing to a whole operating television station, get all the equipment installed and everything ready
to go, between the end of July and September 11th? You
don't. But we did."

Partly it was a result of superb planning while they waited for the thirty-day construction permit. "We did get permission from the Commission to pour the cement for the building we had to put under the tower, because that takes the longest to harden. But for the rest, while we waited, we tore everything out from the interior of the Caterpillar building and had all the material ordered and stockpiled and ready to go into place the minute the thirty days were up."

"And all the while," I said, "I seem to recall that Clancy and the *Herald* were saying that it was impossible for you to meet the September deadline."

"That's right," said Leo Beranek in his calm, quiet way. "They kept calling us liars and using that word practically every day on the front page of their newspaper. And then, just at the end of August, something happened that threw us into a tailspin from which we almost didn't recover."

What happened was that at this critical moment one piece of the mud Clancy had continually thrown at them stuck!

Nathan David was one of the original movers of BBI and one of its largest stockholders. A lawyer who had at one time worked for the FCC, he was particularly useful in dealings with that body and in fact was generally credited with having written the "perfect paper" detailing BBI's high-minded purpose and ideals.

There seems no question of Nathan David's own high ideals, but his sense of what a lawyer is permitted to do may have been somewhat careless, although certainly nothing more nefarious.

The case in point concerned his involvement with a company called Synergystics, of which he was general counsel and which he thought had a very promising future; four of his friends thought so too and wanted to buy a block of stock. Could David sell it to them at slightly less than the over-the-counter price? David agreed to do this and told his four friends that for his services he would charge them a dollar for each share he sold them.

Leo Beranek reports: "What Clancy found out was that Nathan David had violated the criminal statutes of this state because in charging these people a dollar a share he had acted as a broker without a broker's license."

David was outraged, insisting that he had acted as a lawyer and billed as a lawyer; if he had charged them a fee of $684 instead of a dollar a share, there would have been no problem. But now there was. The attorney general, a close friend of Clancy's, took it to the Grand Jury, which indicted David for a criminal offense. And that came close to really sinking things for BBI.

It was truly a desperate situation for them as the scene shifted once more back to Washington and to an FCC now under the chairmanship of Nixon appointee Dean Burch, who had every reason to want to keep Republican media influence strong in Boston. Among the rumors flying was talk that Nixon himself was "taking an interest," that Dean Burch had been consulting with Charles Colson at the White House and had in fact been told to seek a remand, in other words a request that the case be returned to the FCC for a new (and obviously different) decision, and at the same time to rescind the construction permit awarded to BBI.

Against this dreadful possibility BBI prepared a crucial letter pointing out that what the FCC contemplated doing would destroy them, that they had already spent millions of dollars on construction that was, according to an affidavit from Leo Beranek, 95 percent completed. How could the FCC even consider forfeiting this huge investment on the basis of mere allegations of wrongdoing on the part of one stockholder?

However, just to ensure that no further delays would occur, BBI would separate Nathan David from the board entirely until he was fully cleared.

This letter, plus the strong support of the newest and youngest of the FCC commissioners, Nick Johnson, carried the day, at least to a degree. The construction permit was not rescinded; BBI was permitted to proceed "at its own peril." And the FCC's request for a remand went to the Court of Appeals, which promptly turned it down. The Supreme Court also declined to hear the same sorry story again.

Meanwhile, of course, the September start-up date had long since passed, and Clancy, pretending and perhaps actually feeling confidence, continued to buy time by instituting another Court-of-Appeals-to-Supreme-Court go-around.

This time the Court of Appeals, in passing the ball back to the FCC, again ruled that "the interest of justice would not be furthered by recalling the case."

So now it was finally up to the FCC, which voted over the most bitter objections of Dean Burch to grant BBI a start-up date of March 19, 1972. And the mystery of this chapter was that in the end Dean Burch, apparently seeing the tide running against him, reversed himself and cast his vote in favor of BBI.

There was still the Supreme Court, however, and Harold Clancy in one last do-or-die attempt, six days before the agreed-upon start-up date, enlisted the good offices of Abe Fortas, former member of the Court, to try to persuade his onetime brethren to grant certiorari—in other words, finally to rehear this interminable case.

And now indeed BBI was truly down to the wire. Although their start-up date granted by the FCC was on Sunday, March 19, they could not actually go on the air until the last resort—the Supreme Court—upheld the date by refusing to rehear the case.

If by some dreadful mischance the "nine old men" were persuaded by Fortas's alchemy to reconsider once more, the delay, even if the outcome was again favorable—would mean the death knell for BBI.

Because by then they were severely in debt; the bank had understandably refused to lend them another penny until they had a picture on the tube, and their creditors, most of whom had been put off since September, were clamoring ever more insistently. All the key men on the board had mortgaged everything—houses, cars, anything that would bring them more money—to keep their dream alive.

By the Friday before the Sunday start-up date, there was still no word from their operative in Washington, Don Ward, monitoring the Supreme Court.

Says Leo Beranek, "We had to sit with the specter of bankruptcy on that terrible day. If the Court had not approved the Sunday start-up date, all of us, and our wives sitting at home, faced the loss of practically everything we owned."

At five o'clock in the afternoon Ward called from Washington to say that the clerk of the Supreme Court had just informed him that the Court was about to adjourn for the weekend, probably without considering their case.

This was the pit—the actual bottom of despair. Could they dare go on the air on Sunday without this final okay?

Then, by the grace of God and of justice, the phone rang again. Don Ward was back. And Leo Beranek, that calmest, most balanced, most controlled of men, dropped the phone and screamed to all within the sound of his voice, "WE'RE ON THE AIR!"

It seems appropriate here to follow that triumphant announcement with a brief who's who of some of the key members of the BBI board.

Leo Beranek, president of the company, who has already been introduced, is a Harvard Ph.D. who was given a ten-

WCVB, Channel 5 BBI management team: (left to right)
Robert Bennett, Vice President/General Manager, Operations;
Matthew Brown, Chairman of the Board, BBI; Dr. Leo
Beranek, President, BBI; Richard Burdick, Vice President/
General Manager, Creative Services; and Thomas Maney,
Vice President/Assistant General Manager, Director of Sales

ured professorship at MIT and made director of their acoustical lab at the age of thirty-three. He is co-founder of the
consulting firm of Bolt, Beranek, and Newman, which became one of the most noted acoustical computer, information
science, and communications technology companies in the
country. "Most of my life," says Beranek "has been spent
dealing with people who create things."

One of the progenitors of BBI, Judge Matthew Brown,
chairman of the board, is a lawyer who served for a time as
a special justice in the Boston Municipal Court. A prominent
public servant, he has been a trustee of the Combined Jewish
Philanthropies, the American Jewish Committee, and Beth

Israel Hospital, and a member of the Board of Selectmen in his native Brookline, Massachusetts.

It was Judge Brown who first recruited William Pourvu, a young economist, a real estate expert, now teaching at the Harvard Business School, and Leo Beranek, who latched onto him to be his second in command, "combining my experience with his vigor," and persuaded him to devote half time to the station.

The late John H. Knowles, famed doctor, professor, and administrator, onetime director of the Massachusetts General Hospital and, until his death in 1979, president of the board of trustees of the Rockefeller Foundation, was one of BBI's best-known directors.

Oscar Handlin, distinguished American historian, Pforzheimer University professor and director of the Charles Warren Center for Studies in American History at Harvard, winner of the Pulitzer Prize and many other awards for his prolific and trenchant writings, was an active participant in the operation of the station.

Jordan Baruch, vice-president of Bolt, Beranek, and Newman, professor of electrical engineering at MIT and of business administration first at the Harvard Business School and subsequently at the Amos Tuck School of Business Administration at Dartmouth, brought expertise both in science and business to the board.

Other distinguished members included Robert Gardner, anthropologist at Harvard and avant-garde filmmaker; Gerald Holton, physicist at Harvard, writer, and editor; William Andres, lawyer, trustee of numerous educational institutions, and chairman of the board of trustees at Dartmouth College; and F. Stanton Deland, chairman of the Board of Overseers at Harvard.

The goal of these men and their colleagues was to make creative and stimulating use of what they considered a great medium. If it would one day make those who invested in

BBI rich (or richer), that was not the first thing on their minds as they began their television careers.

During these pre-start-up months of travail, Bob Bennett was having some different and difficult problems of his own in the matter of a network affiliation. BBI's pledge of fifty hours a week of local broadcasting was not sitting at all well with the networks, which, as Bennett puts it, "want to program your station from sign-on to sign-off." In many cases, even today, they come close to achieving that goal, often airing a mere ten local hours a week—perhaps sometimes as "much" as fifteen.

WHDH had been a CBS station, but that network was not about to deal with fifty hours and the possibility of being preempted all the time. So CBS made a commitment to Channel 7, at that time an RKO station in Boston and an ABC affiliate. The other Boston VHF station, Channel 4, was solidly tied to NBC.

Forced out of Channel 7, ABC was left without a Boston affiliate, except the possibility of BBI, with which they were reluctant to "jump into bed" because of the large number of local live hours. So they stalled—for three months they stalled, until Bennett had had enough.

His trump card was that if ABC didn't affiliate with them, they would have had to go with a UHF station in Boston, and because UHFs usually have a weaker signal, it is axiomatic that it is more difficult to succeed financially with a U than with a V station.

With this in mind, Bennett called Elton Rule, then president of ABC, and put it to him: "You've been playing games with us, but now I've got to know. If you don't sign with us today, I'm going to declare us an independent VHF station. And if I do that, you're going to have the toughest grind you ever had in your life, first because I *know* how to run an independent station, and second because then ABC will be left with a UHF in the sixth largest market in the country."

Here he left Elton Rule to draw his own somber conclusions, which he promptly did. An hour later he called Bennett back. ABC would be happy to have BBI, if and when BBI went on the air, as an affiliate.

This contretemps took place during the summer of 1971, when all negotiations were geared to the September start-up date. Equally pressing was the matter of acquiring a staff ready to man the station, now called WCVB,† the moment it went on the air. Bennett had hired a number of first-rate men and women. Personnel, salespeople, a program manager, technical people, a public relations director, and a news director came on board—and on salary—during the summer, but there was still the matter of the "talent" to be solved.

WHDH had four very good newscasters that the new BBI coveted, and unfortunately so did the RKO General station Channel 7. In fact RKO had already made these men an offer for the moment WHDH went off the air and was about to announce the coup at a press conference when Beranek and Bennett moved in on them.

Beranek takes credit for the maneuver; Bennett, he says, thought they were too late, but was persuaded to go along when, at the eleventh hour, they took sportscaster Don Gillis and newsman Jack Hynes, certainly the two top men in the city, to lunch.

"We don't want you to go to a second-rate station like Channel 7," Beranek recalls saying. "It's a kind of sleazy operation, and here we've got the best general manager in the country."

Bennett, while probably making appropriately modest noises, did not disagree. And in fact Beranek was correct to

†Note the juxtaposition of these three letters on the bottom row of typewriter keys.

lead off his sales pitch with the virtues of his general manager, who in the eyes of Boston television looked like the only person in the whole BBI operation who knew his way around the business. The rest were widely regarded as a bunch of well-meaning do-gooders who knew absolutely nothing about running a television station and had little going for them except some far-out, impractical ideas. But Bennett's track record gave the two newsmen pause. He had been sales manager of KTTV, Los Angeles, general manager of WTTG, Washington, and when he was hired away by BBI he had for several years been general manager of WNEW, New York.

Beranek and his colleague, Bill Pourvu, vice-president of BBI, had lured Bennett away from this prestigious job (complete with limousine and driver) by offering him equity: 5 percent of the company, in fact, which by Bennett's own estimate, since he figured a station in the Boston market was probably worth $50 million at that time, made his share two and a half million.

Bennett and Beranek now held out this same bait—equity in the company at ten dollars a share—to Jack Hynes and Don Gillis, though not of course in the same amount, with the same positive results. "Those two were the stars," said Beranek. "Once we got them, their colleagues John Henning and Chet Curtis, who were the second echelon but whom we also wanted, came along, also on the agreement that they could buy stock at ten dollars a share."

They now had the four top people from WHDH as a nucleus, and when they finally went on the air it was with Jack Hynes and John Henning at the 6:00 P.M. and 11:00 P.M. news anchor desk, Don Gillis on sports at these hours, and Chet Curtis as weekend anchor man.

Actually there was a silver-lining department in the September-to-March start-up delay. During that period which Bennett refers to as the twilight zone, quite a number of significant things happened. For one thing, WCVB was permitted by the FCC to test its signal during the two hours that WHDH was off the air in the early hours of the morning and to clear up many technical bugs. Organizational foulups were straightened out, the building began working for them, and, perhaps most valuable, the staff already on hand was able to get some very important shows taped and ready to go on the air.

Prominent among these was *Jabberwocky*, a half-hour children's program combining live hosts with animated segments, music, and children's art, which BBI's young producers made on film for only $5,000 an episode. Bennett with his characteristic zeal calls it "the most significant show for kids ever made." Hyperbole aside, there is no question that *Jabberwocky*'s airing between 7:00 and 7:30 A.M. every weekday did get WCVB off to a wonderful start. It was quickly spotted by the influential Action for Children's Television (ACT), a watchdog outfit intent on improving programming for kids, as a program of special character and cited as evidence that the new station was really sincere about producing quality programming.

There was ample other evidence pointing to the new station's determination that profit remain always secondary to quality and public service. On the very first day, for example, they launched Dr. Timothy Johnson, a discovery of Dr. John Knowles, in a program called *Medical Call*, which was on four mornings a week and then spun out to include a weekly evening show called *House Call*. Before long, they also started doing prime-time specials.

In May 1972, after they'd been on the air less than two months, they did a program, preempting prime time (as ABC had feared), on racial imbalance in Boston public schools, an imbalance that led two years later to the controversial court order of Judge W. Arthur Garrity mandating school desegregation by busing.

Dr. Timothy Johnson

A bit later in 1972 Channel 5 did a two-hour special called *To Live in New England*, aimed at children and portraying the varied charms of the area in which they were growing up, and an hour special called *So Frail a Thing* that detailed the many threats to the Massachusetts environment.

The year 1973 saw many more prime-time specials. One, called *Symphony*, was a documentary about the Boston Symphony Orchestra and its then-new director, Seiji Ozawa. Another, *No Fish Tomorrow*, dealt with the crisis in the New England fishing industry, and yet another focusing on air travel in and out of Boston was called *How Safe Is Logan Airport?* (Answer: Not very.)

In one of the first of many school desegregation specials, called *Busing: A Tale of Two Cities*, a WCVB crew went to San Francisco, which had just gone through court-ordered busing, and compared its experience with the pending Boston one. As it turned out, San Francisco's experience was a good deal more orderly than Boston's tumultuous public-school upheaval.

Possibly the preemption which created the most attention in those early years was the start of what would eventually be a whole series of medical documentaries featuring Dr. Tim Johnson. This one, dealing with heart attacks, was called *The Frightening Feeling You're Going to Die*. It cost $100,000 to produce and was the first preemption which not only received attention outside of Boston (it was eventually syndicated and ran in most major markets) but also stunned everyone by coming in first in the ratings in the time period against CBS and NBC shows.

These, to be sure, were only a sampling of the station's prime-time specials. Other local programs running in non–prime time (hours known throughout the industry as Daytime, Early Fringe, Prime Access, and Late Fringe) tried to provide diversity and present a lot of different showcases for different portions of the viewing audience. For example, one of the station's most eclectic hours ran at two in the morning when Robert Gardner regularly carried on a colloquy with various avante-garde filmmakers for the benefit of arty insomniacs.

Still airing with some success today is one program from those early days, *Good Day*, a live morning talk and entertainment show, and from later in the 1970s, *Miller's Court*, with Harvard Law School professor Arthur Miller.

In the early 1970s the very idea of even *having* editorials was a brand-new concept. WCVB carried a daily editorial often written and read by Oscar Handlin, who took over as chairman of the editorial board and added distinction to this facet of the operation.

Gradually the industry began to take note of this station (which most entrenched broadcasters had not at first taken very seriously) if for no other reason than that they were so boldly and often preempting network prime time for public affairs programs, a heretofore unheard-of procedure.

As Bennett explains, "Normally locals would preempt the

network to make money. They would knock out a movie that the network was running to put in their own movie. That way they would keep all the revenue. So if ABC put on a movie at nine in the evening, it would mean maybe five thousand dollars to the local on an hourly rate. But if the local put on their own movie and preempted the network, they might do thirty-five to forty-five thousand dollars. So the tendency is for the station to want to preempt the network and for the network not to want them to.

"However, in our case what made it difficult for ABC was the *kind* of shows we were preempting for. We'd call and say, 'We're going to do a program on the emerging consciousness of fatherhood [*Babies Are for Fathers Too*] or on a profile of a lifer in Framingham Prison for Women. We're probably going to spend a hundred thousand dollars to do this and we expect to lose about seventy-five thousand. But even so, we think it's important for the community.

"The network obviously couldn't fight that. And then, as we started preempting more and more programs, and as so many of them won their time period, suddenly the image of the station started to spread out all over the country. ABC was unhappy about the preemptions, but at the same time ABC was proud."

However, if anyone has the impression that, despite their auspicious start, everything was smooth sailing during those first few years he or she should be quickly disabused.

Participants' memories of the difficulties encountered vary. Leo Beranek thinks back to dealing with a great deal of hostility in the community because of the widely held belief that it was his station that was responsible for closing down the *Herald Traveller*, which many people in Boston had grown up with and still sorely missed. And though the newspaper was losing so much money that it would have closed anyway, WCVB was blamed from throwing some two thousand people out of work.

Bob Bennett recalls how during the first year they had some staff morale problems. "A number of people were unhappy, and I'd say to them, 'This doesn't make any sense. Here we are doing all these wonderful new programs, and you're unhappy. I can't believe it.' Then it dawned on me. Many of the staff had never worked in television before; they had nothing to compare us to. But when some of them eventually moved on to other stations in New York or Chicago or wherever, they would write back to their friends at Channel 5 and say, 'My God, we didn't know it then, but CVB was Camelot.'"

Camelot always looms large in Bennett's perceptions of WCVB, as does his often repeated contention that, despite some fleeting unhappiness among the inexperienced staff, *"there was no fear of failure here.* People would come to me with an idea and I would kill myself trying to find reasons why we could do it. So then they would go to the news department or the program department and say, 'Bob Bennett listened to what I suggested, and we're going to do the show.' And that attitude spread all over the building."

Diametrically opposed is Oscar Handlin's recollection, possibly explained by his more saturnine nature as opposed to Bennett's exuberant one. But for whatever reason, Handlin remembers that when they started to recruit a staff, people from all over the country who had jobs in TV stations, but were sick of the standard fare they were producing, wrote to them. "We had the pick of the crop. Really experienced professionals."

But this, he believes proved something of a disadvantage. "We had a program advisory board made up of producers, assistant producers, directors, writers, cameramen, technicians, all of whom were so deeply rooted in standard television procedures that they were unable to implement the concepts we had in mind. We would have an innovative idea we wanted to try out, and they would say, 'It won't work.

It's too expensive.' So Pourvu or Brown or Beranek would say to them, 'It doesn't matter how much it costs.' But still they had the idea of a rigid budget too firmly ingrained. So we were never able to make the fundamental changes from the top down to the working level."

Bill Pourvu, reconciling these disparate views (a role he must have played often during the BBI days), says both men are in a sense correct, because BBI *did* have to staff its station differently from most stations in order to have enough variety of workers to produce programs with such diverse perspectives. And so they had a combination of people. Many were inexperienced, as Bennett asserts, because there was no standard market they could draw from. Other stations simply weren't doing their sort of programming. But then, as WCVB progressed, professionals who, as Handlin says, were excited at the ideas emanating from this new station and were eager to get involved signed on. Yet they were perhaps not quite ready to accept the bottom-line-is-*second* philosophy.

Nonetheless the fact is that BBI never from its inception actually lost money. Even in the partial start-up year of 1972 they cleared $800,000. But what they made in those early years was a pittance compared with the other two VHF stations in the city.

For instance, according to Bennett, who slings figures around with abandon while others consider profits and cash flow as hush-hush as the KGB, Channel 5 made $1.6 million in 1973, while Channel 4 WBZ was making $10 million and Channel 7, "which wasn't even doing anything halfway decent," made $9 million. But WCVB kept creeping up, and by 1976 everything turned golden for them.

First syndication began to pay off. *Good Day!*, the morning talk show, was playing in seventy-one markets, *Jabberwocky* in ninety-one, and *House Call* in eighty-five. But the most notable during this period was a popular weekly show called *The Baxters*, which dealt with social issues as seen through the eyes of a nice liberal family, the antithesis of the Archie Bunkers. *The Baxters* ran in syndication with Norman Lear for two years. Lear incidentally referred to WCVB as the best commercial television station in America‡ and to Bob Bennett as the best local broadcaster in the country.

Furthermore, by 1976 the promised fifty hours of local broadcasting had gone up to sixty-two hours, more than those of any other network affiliate in the country.

Then, in May 1976, Channel 5 was given tangible recognition by winning the highly esteemed George Foster Peabody Award, always before given to a specific program but never, as in this case, to a station for overall excellence.

In July, when the Queen of England came to Boston, sportingly to help her country's former colony celebrate its freedom, WCVB was the only station in Boston to cover her appearance toe to toe on Massachusetts soil. The broadcast, lasting some eight hours, was a big plus for Channel 5. Among other things, it was notable locally for linking Natalie Jacobson, already a star, with Chet Curtis. Chet, however, seems to remember above all that he had a terrible backache and could not get to the bathroom once during the eight hours they were on the air nonstop.

Another fortuitous circumstance for CVB was that ABC had hit their stride and shot to the top of the network ladder by first covering the 1976 Summer Olympics and then, later in that season, producing the immensely popular dramatization of Alex Haley's *Roots*.

All these factors built up to such a pitch that, as Bennett puts it, "the money started coming in so fast we couldn't get out of the way of it."

"Was anyone ducking?" I asked him.

"Yes, as a matter of fact, the board was. I would have

‡Boston also has what most consider to be the best Public Broadcasting station— WGBH, Channel 2—in America.

expected any other company to give me a standing O for managing a station that was making so much money, but this board acted honest-to-God *embarrassed*. I guess they figured that if it was making all that money it couldn't be quality."

I observed (silently) that one way or another the BBI board had managed rather handily within the next few years to overcome its embarrassment of riches.

No one can pinpoint just when the thought of selling their brainchild first came to members of the BBI board. At first glance it seems impossible to imagine that they could have even entertained such an idea after all they had been through, first to acquire the license and second to make the station such a widely acclaimed success and such a financial bonanza.

But the truth is that the very reason selling the station seemed so improbable was the very reason that sentiment to do so began to build. The fact that it had taken them ten long years from gleam in the eye to start-up meant that many of the board members who had been in their fifties when negotiations with the FCC first started were in their seventies in 1980 and were, in the words of Leo Beranek, starting to say, " 'Well, what happens to my stock if I die?' We had no public market. It was all still privately held. There's no way that anyone else on the board was going to come up with several million dollars for my stock, so I and the dozen other men on the board who had large holdings would have had to go outside and make what would amount to a bargain sale."

I inquired how much of a "bargain" a bargain sale would actually have been.

Beranek looked at me squarely. "You couldn't sell it for what it was worth. No way."

"Even so—" I started to say, but he cut me off: "I'd say you'd probably have gotten a fourth of the amount of money."

Even so, I again wanted to ask, since the ball-park figure Beranek was rumored to have made from the sale of the station was $13 million, wouldn't $3 million plus still have been a nice little windfall, enough to compensate for keeping the long-sought-for ideal of local ownership and participation alive? Could not those who felt it necessary to sell possibly have accepted a ready buyer even at the reduced price and let a partnership of younger men and the employees, none of whom wanted to sell, carry on?

Apparently not. The vote of the board, which consisted largely of the dozen or so men with the largest holdings and therefore the greatest concern about the sale of stock by estates after their deaths, was strongly in favor of selling the station. And when the question was put to all the stock-holders, according to Beranek, they were overwhelmingly in favor of unloading BBI for the most money they could get, still consistent with quality broadcasting.

Exactly how Metromedia qualified for the second half of that equation is hard to fathom. Certainly their reputation, as Bennett once said in an unguarded moment, was as a company that featured reruns of *I Love Lucy* for the seventeenth time, a company that was considered unimaginative, interested only in making as much money as possible and doing as little as possible to accomplish it.

But Bennett honestly believed, and not without justification, that if he brought WCVB to Metromedia and himself went back to work for John Kluge as president of the television company, he could not fail to improve the character of the other six stations in Dallas, Houston, Washington, New York, Chicago, and Los Angeles. Furthermore, Bob Bennett had dreams, apparently shared by Kluge, who, it is said, looked upon him as a son, to transform these stations into the core of a fourth network.

And as for BBI, what moved them toward Metromedia was simply that the price was right. The only other companies contacted, Gannett Publishers and the *Los Angeles Times* (Hearst was incidentally not even considered), made offers far below Metromedia's $220 million.

And so the deed was done. The station was sold to John Kluge in July 1981; the deal was consummated in May 1982 when the telephone operators began answering, "Channel 5, Metromedia."

There is a tendency on the part of many to denigrate Metromedia's ownership of Channel 5 just because of what Metromedia was perceived to be as a company. But in fact their contribution was considerable, albeit far more material—they poured $5 million into expansion and improvement of the station—than in any real programming creativity. But even in that area, thanks in part perhaps to Bob Bennett's making his headquarters at WCVB in the beginning, they can truthfully be said to have held the line, if not greatly expanded its reach.

Their ambitious building program included a brand-new studio complete with its own control room (heretofore the station had had only one studio besides the Newsroom), now the largest commercial studio in New England, comparable to any in the larger New York, Chicago, or Los Angeles markets. In addition they added an entire new floor, very grand indeed, to house the corporate offices of Metromedia Television and Radio, of which Bob Bennett was now president.

Bennett was trying to keep his finger on the pulse of his beloved CVB even while his duties had enlarged to include all six of the other Metromedia stations. He argued in favor of the Boston headquarters for his company on the grounds that he was tired of seeing palm trees in every situation comedy coming out of Hollywood and saw no reason why, given the new studio, they couldn't just as well produce sitcoms in Boston.

When I made my first sortie to Needham to investigate the possibility of writing this book it was just two years into the Metromedia regime. Everyone insisted—in hindsight, perhaps they protested too much—that nothing had really changed except for the better. Besides the new building program, $2 million had been spent to bring all the equipment up to state-of-the-art levels. Specials preempting prime time, while somewhat fewer in number than they had been in the beginning, still continued to be produced when the situation warranted.

A notable success had been the station's original production, just before the Metromedia sale, of *Summer Solstice*, starring Henry Fonda, in his last performance, and Myrna Loy. Certainly this was an unusual coup for a local television station, and Metromedia (Bennett) promptly picked up the skein and announced the inception of a new series of one-hour original dramatic shows to be called Metromedia Playhouse. (There have been two so far.)

So there was progress, yes, but still the place had a different, a corporate feeling. Somehow no one was talking about Camelot, and here and there one could pick up traces of nostalgia for the good old BBI days when they were a family, a big overgrown Mom-and-Pop store of a television station on a roll.

It is October 1985. WCVB is still in limbo. Until Hearst takes over after the new year, the operators continue to answer, "Channel 5, Metromedia." But Metromedia in the person of Bob Bennett has gone.

A month earlier the staff officially bade him farewell in a touching little ceremony that featured a nostalgic video tape highlighting Bennett's eventful years. In the words of Jim Coppersmith, the master of ceremonies, to Bennett, "We believe this film, put together over the weekend, captures pretty much what this place has accomplished and *will* ac-

complish . . . and, most of all, has your smudgy little finger-
prints all over it. So let's hope now we'll have a perfect roll
cue and great audio."

It need hardly be added that the audio was—what else—
the singing of "Camelot," its "fleeting glimpse of glory" in-
terspersed with Bob Bennett's own voice repeating his conviction that "every station in the country should devote a
substantial portion of its revenue to locally produced television beyond the news."

Then the topper. Coppersmith called Bennett to the po-
dium and, after graceful encomia to his friend of many years
for his "charisma combined with a vulnerability born of a
deep sense of caring," announced that the building would
henceforth be known as the Bennett Building and presented
him with a plaque, now affixed to the front door, reading:

The Bennett Building. Named for Robert M. Bennett
in recognition of his inspirational and visionary leadership as founding general manager of WCVB TV.

Bennett who describes himself as "a mush face" ("I cry
when I give away a pair of old shoes"), got through his
acceptance speech dry-eyed and told his devoted followers,
"Magic dust was sprinkled on this building, this station, and
all its people." He also managed his favorite reference to "no
fear of failure here" and adroitly passed the wand to Hearst
by saying that Frank Bennack, president of the company,
looked on this station as its Hope diamond.

So, we shall see.

Meanwhile, business as usual.

3

Daytime I: The *Eyeopener*, 5:30 to 7:00 A.M.

"**I**F I WERE WRITING A book like yours," a young staffer at WCVB volunteered to me one morning, "I'd begin at the start of the day and go through every local program we do."

By coincidence, I told him, that indeed was my very idea.

"Which means," he added with a malicious grin, "getting up at four in the morning one day to see the station start up with the *Eyeopener* at five-thirty. But," he said, "you've really got to experience it because that program is different from every other hour of the day."

His thought is echoed by Susan Burke, co-anchor of the *Eyeopener*. "No one in their right mind would get up at this terrible hour in the morning unless they really loved their job," she tells me. "You'll have to come out here at that time to see it for yourself to understand it."

Convinced, I get up at four, start out in the pitch dark, and arrive just as the light is breaking through the sky. It is very still. The parking lot is empty. But once inside the windowless, brightly lit Newsroom, I am greeted by cheers for having made it and enveloped by a feeling of collegial warmth.

One can hardly say the station is just waking up at 5:30 on this or any other weekday morning because in fact it has never gone to sleep. But though Channel 5 operates twenty-four hours a day, it does in fact doze off a bit in the period between 1:00 A.M. and daybreak, resting on its laurels with reruns of the previous day's local programs, and usually an old black-and-white movie.

On guard during this gray period are four stalwarts: the Master Controller, who pushes the buttons that send the signal from the station to the viewing audience, the producer of the upcoming live 5:30 A.M. *Eyeopener News*, the writer for that show, and an overnight video-tape editor. These four people are wide awake.

Producer Leetha Yee and writer Rose Lewis have started their working "day" at 11:00 P.M., observing the late news at that hour. Many of the stories from that half-hour program will as a matter of course be repeated on the *Eyeopener*.

Meanwhile, throughout the night Cable News Network (CNN) is recorded and taped hour by hour, and any important developing national stories are readied for 5:30 A.M. In addition, AP and UPI feed a steady stream of computer printouts of stories which may or may not be of importance to the station.

At the same time, WCVB, in common with all other news facilities in the area, both electronic and print, has a police scanner turned up loud in the assignment room just off the Newsroom to keep Producer Yee abreast of breaking local stories (murders, rapes, fires). These are usually covered and fed into the station by stringer cameramen who have scanners in their cars or, if warranted, by an unhappily awakened WCVB cameraman and reporter.

By 1:30 or 2:00 Leetha Yee is usually able to do a preliminary formatting ("a prelim") of how the first half-hour of her ninety-minute *Eyeopener* is going to run, always allowing time slots for late-breaking news. Rose Lewis is at work writing lead-ins and text for the anchors, and Dave Buehl, veteran ENG (Electronic News Gathering) man, is busily editing video materials.

The stage is thus set for the ungodly hour of 4:30 A.M. when everything begins to gear up and the huge Newsroom comes alive, the only oasis of light and normality in an otherwise dark and inert building.

The feature, having the Newsroom and the set in one large room, is unusual if not unique. Most TV stations have their newsrooms down the hall, or even on another floor apart from the studio, and almost none has a set in which the control room is clearly visible in any long shot.

The anchor desk, which looks deceptively simple when seen on the tube, is in fact quite complex. A round table with five half-moon spaces for five anchor chairs, it is designed to be shot from any side of the studio— front, back, right, or left. In addition, the entire desk can rotate if necessary, making it in effect television in the round.*

Several different "NewsCenter 5" signs are in strategic positions on the walls for background shots. Theatrical lighting is overhead, trippable wires are everywhere, ladders lean against walls, and three giant cameras on dollies stand at the ready, looking like one-eyed robots.

To the left as one faces the set is the weatherman's glassed-in room, and next to that is the green screen on which he *pretends* to be pointing to the various sections of the United States. Actually the screen remains totally blank during his broadcasts as he reads the map from the end of the camera,

---

*This is the way the studio and anchor desk looked when I wrote this chapter. But like so much at WCVB, "all things change except the love of change." Therefore, see Chapter 5 for an update.

Susan Burke and Jim Boyd at pod

Susan Burke and Jim Boyd

making it something of a trick to hit, let's say, the Ohio Valley with his pointer on the empty screen behind him and not one of the plains states.

In the Newsroom proper are the three cloverleaf tables—"pods"—each with five bays containing a desk, typewriter, telephone, and, in the wide common center part, all the expected paraphernalia, dictionaries, thesauruses, old and new scripts, newspapers, computer printouts, and half-drunk Styrofoam cups of coffee. Wastebaskets overflow, and broken typewriters are strewn about the floor, some with an irritable note attached to the platen: "This typewriter keeps jumping five spaces"; "This typewriter has no letter *A*."

Numerous little glassed-in hutches, all equally over-crowded, shoot off from the main room; on one wall is a bank of television sets, one tuned to Cable News Network and the others to different local stations so that a wary eye can be kept on what the competition is up to.

Each pod belongs to a different news hour, and at four-thirty in the morning the pod nearest the entrance to the Newsroom fills up and becomes the nerve center for the people, few in number, but potent in intent, who in one hour are going to put the first news program on the air.

First there are the two anchors: handsome, impeccably dressed Jim Boyd, extremely popular with his fellow workers because of his high professional qualities, his intelligence, and genial, thoughtful manner; and Susan Burke, with her engaging looks, pleasing voice, and easygoing competence.

Susan is eight and three-quarters months pregnant with her first child. In fact, half the women on the staff seem to be pregnant ("It's the water" has become the favorite cliché), and all are determined to hang on until the last moment. Natalie Jacobson, anchor of the 6:00 and 11:00 P.M. shows, set the standard by practically going into labor during the six o'clock news. But to the disappointment of her colleagues, Susan Burke lasted out her full work week and decorously had her baby boy on a Saturday when none of them could enjoy the drama.

Bob Copeland, the weatherman, usually comes in well before four-thirty in order to have time to study the meteorological maps which are transmitted by phone line from the National Weather Bureau in Washington and to read them into his computer. He also checks with numerous of his thirty well-deployed weather watchers to make up a weather-watch map showing temperatures and weather conditions throughout the New England area.

Lest everyone seem to be coming across as just too happy and contented on the *Eyeopener*-to-*Midday* shift, I am almost relieved to be able to report that Bob Copeland is not at all fond of early-morning hours. He is a night person, he says, and when he was moved from the six and eleven o'clock news to the *Eyeopener* and *Midday* it played havoc with his life, and although he has gradually adjusted, he still is not exactly dewy-eyed about his time slot.

Phil Levy, producer of the *Midday News*, arrives. A large, bluff, bark-is-worse-than-his-bite old pro, Levy sees that the tapes for the *Eyeopener* are properly edited, helps Leetha Yee line them up, and consults with her about the final formatting of the show.

As Jim and Susan and Levy take their places at the *Eyeopener-Midday* pod, which is now full with Yee and writer Lewis at the other two spots, the technical crew is also checking in. Isaac Laughinghouse is control-room director for the 5:30–6:00 segment. Jim Lowell directs the 6:00–7:00 segment. The audio man who sits in a glassed-in sound proof booth inside the glassed-in control room is Jim Barker. Caroline Stallings, who has multiple jobs, first types the Chyrons (all the printed words that appear on the screen on a machine that operates like a word processor). She then takes on the very responsible task of seeing that each camera has its teleprompter in place and rolling at the correct speed.

All these people are members of the International Brotherhood of Electrical Workers; they are regulars in the "headset circuit" of the *Eyeopener* and *Midday News*, each being connected to the sound of Laughinghouse's or Lowell's voice as they give the cues and commands from the control room. Other members of the headset circuit are the three cameramen and the floor manager, who cues in the anchors and controls them with hand signals.

Jim Boyd and Susan Burke most often start out their working day by writing the 6:30–7:00 part of the show, which because of understaffing at that hour has not received much attention. Unless there are important late-breaking stories, it does not vary greatly from the earlier segments, but still it must be written out and timed.

Everyone uses large-type typewriters, which allow only about fifty or sixty words a page. And a page is not just a page, but a packet of six sheets with carbons in between. When the text is complete, the copies are distributed. Jim gets the yellow sheet, Susan the pink, the control-room director the orange, producer green, the teleprompter operator the blue, and the audio man the white.

As 5:30 approaches, even though they all go through the same routine each weekday, it is still not cut-and-dried. Tension mounts. Typewriters bang furiously, sheets of colored paper are rushed back and forth to accommodate last-minute changes.

Rose Lewis to Susan Burke: "Do you have the new page 32A?" Leetha Yee to Phil Levy: "But I think it makes more sense to put the fatal accident in Canton before the Expressway story."

Phil Levy agrees and tells Dave Buehl: "Change your ENG order." Although *ENG* stands for "Electronic News Gathering," it is a broad term which in this particular case refers to the three machines that hold the video tapes, arranged in order, for each broadcast. For some incomprehensible reason the machines are numbered 4, 5, and 6. Hence: "Story C on four instead of five. . . . Repeat C on four."

In the control room, Laughinghouse tells Skip Peabody, the switcher next to him, "Change your ESS. [Electronic Still Store is the picture that appears in the corner of the screen over the speaker's shoulder.] Number 1420 now comes before number 1450."

Jim Boyd hurries in from the makeup room and grabs a last cup of coffee as he steps up to the set in shirtsleeves to be "miked." Susan Burke is already in place, her about-to-be-born baby neatly concealed behind the desk.

The lights go on. "Two minutes, stand by," calls the floor manager. Susan and Jim shuffle their papers and make last-minute notations. They of course read from the teleprompter but still need their scripts in case the machine fails. They have not had much chance to read over the material, and each is silently mouthing parts of the script.

I go with Leetha Yee as she slips behind the set to take her place in the control room to the left of Laughinghouse. Peabody the switcher is on his right.

Countdown. "Ten, nine, eight, seven, six, five, four, three, two, one."

Music up. Onto the screen flashes the NewsCenter 5 logo, a blue globe of the world, which fades into a cut of New England. Jim Boyd's and Susan Burke's pictures circle the globe. "Camera two center two shot," says Laughinghouse into his mike.

Jim and Susan are at the anchor desk, the control room visible behind.

"Camera one with effects on Jim," says Laughinghouse.

"Good morning. I'm Jim Boyd, and this is the five-thirty edition of the *Eyeopener*."

"Camera one on Susan."

"And I'm Susan Burke. Topping the news this morning,

two young boys are shot, caught in the crossfire of an argument in Roxbury."

Boyd: "The Bank of Boston holds a news conference this morning."

Burke: "President Reagan goes on national television tonight to support his new budget cuts."

Boyd: "The Red Sox announce they have signed a new left-handed relief pitcher, and Bob Copeland says we'll get some rain today."

These headlines are the tease. We are now ready to go into the first story. "Two Kids shot, ESS 235," says the script. Jim Boyd reads a thirty-four-second "intro." As he comes to the words "Narcisco Rosari is in stable condition at Boston City Hospital," Laughinghouse gives the command, "Roll VC [video cassette] four."

In the ENG room Dave Buehl starts machine four, which takes three seconds to start playing. Boyd finishes, "NewsCenter Five's Ron Gollobin has the details of the shooting." The video tape comes on the screen, and reporter Gollobin's voice is heard over it. The script reads "VC/SOT." Translation: Video Cassette/Sound Over Tape.

The *Eyeopener* is now about two and a half minutes into the broadcast, which will last ninety minutes.

And who, you may ask, is watching at that hour of the morning? Fortunately the television industry has elaborate and sophisticated methods of knowing not only how many people are tuned to a particular station at a particular time, but also their age and sex distribution.

This information, generated by the Nielsen and Arbitron companies, referred to and deferred to ceaselessly as "the numbers," is deceptively complex to grasp, although at first blush it seems easy enough. At least that's what everyone told me as they tried to get me to understand the all important distinction between share and ratings, the two denominators on which "the numbers" are based.

All manner of highly placed executives at the station, plus one or two "talents," took a crack at explaining this mumbo jumbo to me—up to and including Bob Bennett, whose presentation was so confusing that he himself burst out laughing and said, "For God's sake, turn that tape recorder off. If you listen to what I've just told you, you'll never understand it."

Here is a standard definition of the difference between shares and ratings, cribbed from the TV column of the *Boston Globe*. "Ratings tell what percentage of the total TV households in the area are tuned in while shares indicate what percentage of folks already watching TV are tuned in to a particular program." Clear?

Well, then try this one, somewhat fancier and denser, from a Harvard Business School report. "Rating reflected the percentage of all households with TVs that were tuned in to a given program while another measure, called share, reflected the percentage of those TVs that were turned on at a given time that were watching a particular program."

It was Jim Boyd who finally made the breakthrough by writing out the following on his large-print typewriter.

Rating = % of sets turned to Channel 5 . . . of *all sets in the viewing area.*

Share = % of sets tuned to Channel 5 . . . of *all sets turned on at a given time.*

And he illustrated this with drawings of ten little TV sets—the viewing area (in a small hotel)—three with the number 5 written on them, three with the number 7, and four blank. From this he drew the conclusion "Rating = 30% or 3 of 10. Share = 50% or 3 of 6."

There is one more kicker, called Houses Using Television (HUT), which appears in all Arbitron and Nielsen sheets in the first column after the time period and is obviously the same for every station in the entire market in question. That is, "Houses Using Television" means houses using television no matter what station they're tuned to.

And HUT answers the question I first posed before I started out on this chaotic digression, namely, who is watching television at that hour in the morning? The Nielsen HUT tells us that on a given day 7.3 percent of the houses in the viewing area are using television at 5:30 A.M. and that of that number anywhere from 57.5 to 38.5 percent (depending on which day it is and whether it's Arbitron's or Nielsen's numbers) are tuned to the *Eyeopener.*† The HUT figure rises appreciably during the *Eyeopener*'s hour and a half on the air, winding up at 15.1 percent in the last time segment. To place the HUT number in perspective, in prime time the 9:00 P.M. figure is 66.7 percent.

Put in more recognizable terms, the audience consistently tuned in to the *Eyeopener* ranges from 75,000 to 90,000, although Jim Boyd insists that if you include people who are getting up and catching a smidgen of the ninety minutes (Arbitron and Nielsen meters or "diaries" do not rate less than fifteen minutes) the audience would be much greater. So much for the numbers. Sort of.

As to the demographics, also an everyday word in television, they are considered to be "right down the middle," that is, an equal number of viewers in the eighteen-to forty-nine-year-old category as in the over-fifty set. And an even split between male and female.

Here again Jim Boyd is slightly wary of the whole idea of demographics as applied to news programs. "After all," he says, "news is news. Say the demographics tell us that we have a lot of businessmen watching us as they shave. We can't tailor the news just to give them business-oriented stories, or to give the schoolchildren eating their Wheaties kids-oriented stuff. We have to provide infor-

---

†For more on how these figures are gathered, see "Sign-off".

Bob Copeland

mation to people on the basis of what we think are the important stories."

Furthermore, he suggests, "What we really have is a moving audience. People that are getting up and on their way out, housewives with families to get up and get going, and frankly in a lot of cases it may be just 'room tone.' But then there are some people who are pretty much bound to the house and like to get their news from television as they do their chores. There are also a lot of shift workers getting home at four-thirty or five in the morning who don't feel like going right to bed, so they'll sit down with a beer and watch the five-thirty segment."

One thing is certain about the audience, movable or stationary. The thing they care particularly about, especially at that hour of the day, is the weather. Snowsuits for the children? How will that flight to New York be? Raincoat? Umbrella? Take car or use subway? Stay home? All pressing early-morning questions which the *Eyeopener* does its best to answer.

Six times during the program Bob Copeland comes on with his weather reports. Three "long" ones (two and a half minutes) and three quickies (thirty seconds). As with every other facility at this or any other TV station, the weather station carries an array of dauntingly complex-looking apparatus. But under the clear and soothing tutelage of meteorologist Bob Copeland, I found the impossible to understand somehow becoming possible, and what is involved in putting the weather on the air actually fathomable.

Two primary factors: the weatherman's talk is all ad-libbed. What you see on the screen is all done with a special graphic computer into which the WCVB weathermen have stored basic maps which they have sketched and embellished.

So when Copeland arrives at work, after checking his latest weather charts and talking with his spotters, he phones the huge weather computer center in Bedford, Massachusetts, a facility that has access to every sort of teletype and facsimile information that exists. As he puts it, Bedford daily "massages" the data into packages they know each of their subscribers will need. Included and vital in this bundle is the satellite picture, called geo-stationary because the satellite, in orbit at 22,000 miles above the equator, is traveling at the same speed that the Earth is turning, and thus the two bodies appear to be staying in the same spot.

With the satellite information in hand, Copeland then calls up his basic satellite map (one of the ten) to the screen, and the computer superimposes on it the 4:00 A.M. reading from Bedford.

He repeats the same process for the radar map, which, based on a conglomeration of information from about twenty different radar sites, shows in vivid color exactly where there is weather disturbance in the country. Blue indicates light rain, and as it starts to move up through golds into the orange, the weather is worse. At red you're into heavy rain and thunderstorms.

Next Copeland must put "direct acquired information" onto a stored map of the New England area. He calls up a map of the Northeast to read onto it the weather conditions in the various cities in the viewing area (each identified by a three-letter call name like the ones used on airplane baggage checks). Here again the computer understands exactly what to do. Since it knows the latitude and longitude of all of these stations, Copeland simply has to hit the return button on his machine to have it put the weather information— usually only temperature—at the proper locations on the map.

By now it is getting close to air time. Based on all his data he has made his forecast, given it to Caroline Stallings to write on the Chyron machine to appear printed on the screen during his report. This done, he prepares a "show sequence," starting with a base map of the United States which has a little topography and is, as he says, "kind of pretty." Then, using a top-to-bottom wipe, rather like pulling down a window shade, he goes to the satellite map that shows clouds over the pretty map. Next he goes to a conventional map of the United States, annotated with highs, lows, fronts, and other elements associated with weather. And finally he cuts to a close-up of the New England map with its acquired information, and thus he has his sequence. He hits the final "make show sequence" on the computer, puts on his jacket, and gets ready to stand in front of the blank green screen.‡

The computer is attached by cable to the switcher in the

‡The green screen, which is called a Chromakey, used to be blue, but trouble arose with this color. If one of the forecasters happened to be wearing a blue sweater, for example, the satellite map of the United States, clouds and all, would be shown on his sweater as well as on the screen. Hence a color green no one is likely to wear has been chosen.

Dick Albert at the weather "map"

control room, and when the director says, "Okay up on number one," which is the weather's number (just as *wx* is its written signal), the sequence begins. Copeland can change the picture on the screen with a little button he carries; he paces himself by devoting twenty to thirty seconds to each map and comes out in his two-and-a-half-minute allotment.

One further option is available. Channel 5, alone among Boston stations, has its own radar, a dish attached to one of the towers that scans around and around and gives the local weather up to a range of 125 miles. The facility, tied not to the computer but directly to the switcher, can be called up ("Bring up number six") in case bad weather exists or threatens. "Actually," says, Copeland, "we can see a severe thunderstorm coming down the Massachusetts Turnpike and time it minute by minute. So it certainly can be used to the viewers' advantage, and every local station should have one."

One thing always to remember about weathermen: for all the sophisticated state-of-the-art paraphernalia, they wouldn't be able to do their jobs unless they were professional meteorologists trained to interpret the massively complex data they have to work with. Bob Copeland is an MIT graduate; Dick Albert, WCVB's principal weatherman, has his degrees from the University of Michigan.

Meanwhile, in the control room, Jim Lowell is about to take over from Isaac Laughinghouse. During the first half-hour there have been six stories and a quickie marine weather and travel forecast up to the first commercial break. Two long stories and the long weather report plus a traffic report bring us to the second break. During this commercial Susan Burke (or while she is on maternity leave her replacement reporter, Susan Wornick) moves to the six o'clock news pod, hastily cleared of mess, for the "news for the deaf" segment. While she reads about four minutes of news off camera, Derm Keohane sits beside her and hand-signs her words on camera.

This completed, the script reads, "Susan lose Derm, throw to Jim for sports." Jim catches and does three and half minutes of very compressed sports reporting, covering approximately four stories, each accompanied either by a video cassette with his voice-over or by an appropriate picture from the ESS (Electronic Still Store) over his left shoulder.

Next we have one of two or three reports on traffic conditions as covered by the WCVB helicopter, then the inevitable "note of community interest," followed by the tease of what's coming in the next hour.

Something much more than supertechnology, performance, and practiced capability is afoot in this television station at that quiet time of day. There is a quality, a pride, an esprit de corps in the air that is manifest.

Almost no one on the entire staff of Channel 5 gives the impression that he or she is dragging through the daily stint

as if it were just another job. By and large they seem to be
an unusually committed group of people. But on the *Eyeopener* there is a positive *joie de vivre*—a dedication not just
to the station but to each other.

"It's totally different from any other shift I've ever been
on," says Jim Boyd. "We're a really concerned, close-knit
little group of people. Everybody is dedicated to the job, to
the product we put on the air, which we hope is the best in
Boston. But equally we're devoted to our fellow workers. I
think that's the major ingredient of the *Eyeopener*. People
feel that if they don't pull their own weight they're letting
their colleagues down—people that they really get to know
and care about. Even considering the horrendous conditions
under which we work—getting up at three, trying to get to
bed by seven or seven-thirty at night—I think I could take
it for the rest of my career. Because for me it's a first."

"It's great not to have anyone looking over your shoulder,"
says producer Leetha Yee. At that hour, with no chiefs in
sight, the $450 million station is turned over to this tight
little band of Indians.

"I tell you it's fun," says Phil Levy. "We own the place."

On a certain day in May, as we have seen, disturbing
events occurred that caused management and staff alike to
ask the question "Who really *does* own this station?"

But on the *Eyeopener*, on this or any other day, they know.
The station is theirs.

4

Daytime II: *Good Day!*, 10:00 to 11:00 A.M., and *Midday News*, 12:00 to 12:30 P.M.

G$_{OOD\,DAY!}$, THE HARDY perennial of Channel 5, has gone through many transformations in format and style, and in the process a number of dips in popularity. Still it keeps bouncing back, a plucky, feisty, competitive program currently enjoying a modest up.

Dating back to the early BBI epoch, the show was originally called *Good Morning*, until that title, adding the word *America*, was preempted by the station's network affiliate, ABC. As *Good Day!*, it ran from 9:00 to 10:30 A.M, featuring (as it still does) segments of current local news interest, interviews with celebrities, important authors, a potpourri of personalities, and miscellaneous quality-of-life spots varying in interest and pertinence.

In 1973 *Good Day!* was the raison d'être for the creation of a New England Network which carried one hour of the ninety-minute program. The following year WCVB put the first half-hour of the show on tape and sold it to seventy-one stations around the country outside the New England area. Then gradually there began to occur what is referred to in TV circles as "a softening of the numbers," that is, ratings moving downward. Television people are as gifted as anyone I have ever encountered in articulating excuses for this far-from-unusual turn of events. Cited in this case was a "new diversity of alternate programs," notably game shows, serious staff morale problems resulting in a large turnover, and the plain fact that to produce ninety minutes of live television at that hour of the day was not bringing in a big enough dollar return for the effort and studio time involved.

A change was therefore made to move *Good Day!* to 10:00 A.M., to cut it to an hour, and, most drastically, to tape the show rather than run it live, thus removing the flexible spontaneity which was its stock in trade.

Fortunately, after six months in this condition, higher-ups, notably Vice-President for Programming Paul La Camera, interceded and returned *Good Day!* to its proper live status, where it hung on by its fingernails sustained in part by the presence of hostess Eileen Prose, who is still with the show. When a new executive producer of programming, Joseph Heston, came on board, he inherited a *Good Day!* that was regularly hitting the bottom with ratings of 1.

Heston lent his strong support to a young dynamo named Peggy Allen, who—because she came from the number-three market, Chicago, to the number-six market, Boston,—qualified for a high position on the staff of *Good Day!* Within six months, in February 1984, at the age of twenty-six, she became its producer and at once started the show on its upward trend. When I asked Peggy Allen to tell me what she did to bring *Good Day!* back to the world of the living, she said simply, "I opened it up."

"Meaning?"

"They were looking at the topics on the show in a very limited, narrow way that often only appealed to a small part of our listening audiences. *Good Day!* obviously is almost entirely a woman's show at that hour of the day, but the demographics give us a wide spread between all ages of women. Therefore, to lead with a story about osteoporosis, as they had once done, was to bore the younger members of the viewing audience into instant dial turning.

"Or another example which didn't much interest anyone of any age was a piece they led with about the sodium content in seltzer water. Who cares? At least I would have broadened this subject to include all sorts of bottled water plus a few good digs at the snob appeal of Perrier. Even so, it's not a lead. If I used it at all, I'd bury it in the second half close to the end."

The way the show works, there are usually four, sometimes five, segments. At present Peggy Allen tends to lead either with a celebrity—Danny Thomas, Joel Grey, Stephanie Powers, Glenn Close—or often with some sort of titillating piece like Mail-Order Brides, Phone Sex, New York City School for Homosexuals, or Other Women.

The emphasis on the lead, always of primary importance in TV (or in writing of any sort, for that matter), is critical in *Good Day!,* a program which, as Allen puts it, is "topic-driven." So if the viewing audience doesn't cotton to the first topic, even though they have been "teased" several times to let them know what else is coming, they are still likely to switch over to the competition.

Another reason for a strong lead is that *Good Day!* for a long period followed the popular network talk show *Phil Donahue* and therefore had endlessly to strive to carry that highly rated program's numbers into their first half-hour and beyond if possible.*

---

*It did as of this writing. By the end of this book ("Sign-off"), Donahue had moved to the early-fringe hour from 4:00 to 5:00 P.M. and *Good Day!* to his spot at 9:00 instead of 10:00 A.M.

Still, in the ever-present competition for ratings, *Good Day!* consistently runs a point or two behind Channel 4's *People Are Talking* at 12:30 (remember, ratings are the percentage of sets tuned to the channels of all the sets in the viewing area), although it usually beats Channel 4 by four or five points in share (percentage of sets tuned to Channel 4 or 5 of all the sets turned on at a given time). The other talk show, *Morning Live* on Channel 7, which runs at 10:30, is so low in both ratings and shares that it is not really in the ball park.

But there is yet another competition between these morning shows that is if anything more intense than the numbers, and that is the endless struggle to snag the hot celebrities for their programs.

According to Peggy Allen there are various sources for segment topics. First there are people who are making news in town. An example in this category was when Boston was treated to a front-page story about two sisters, one of whom acted as surrogate mother and produced a child for her sterile sister.

Both *Good Day!* and *People Are Talking* were hot on the trail of these two women. *People Are Talking* is a one-topic show, a franchise that is not only offered to Boston viewers but that tours to all Westinghouse stations. Hard to beat. But Joe Heston, egged on by Peggy Allen, persuaded Phil Donahue to book this segment for his show. The sisters wisely preferred the greater exposure of one shot on *Donahue* to the arduous Westinghouse tour, and part of the deal was that they would therefore agree to appear the next day on WCVB. Result: the surrogate sisters appeared one day on *Donahue* and the next on *Good Day!* before *People Are Talking* knew they had been had. So it goes on newsworthy segments of morning talk shows.

All the other types of segments involve somebody trying to promote something—a writer, a film star, a TV personality (an ABC-TV personality that is), someone who has come up with still another "new" diet, a celebrity who has written a book (as distinguished from a writer who has done so), a local department store pushing a fashion line which is visually effective and makes a useful change of pace. Huge conglomerates such a Nestlé's or Pillsbury that package a cook and send him or her around to the talk shows are unacceptable unless their message is couched in some sort of format like, "Let's think of something fun to do with the children on a rainy day, like make cookies."

To book these twenty or more segments a week, Allen has five assistant producers, each of whom both books an individual segment and is responsible for putting together the various elements (which are considerable) needed to get it on the air.

For instance, a recent show was scheduled to lead with actress Glenn Close, who was in town promoting her soon-to-be-released movie *Maxie*. Close did not have time to come to the studio but was glad to shoot a live remote from Boston. To achieve this, Tom Cottle, the show's resident psychologist and co-host, was standing by at the Four Seasons Hotel, where the actress was staying, to interview her, and the sound truck dubbed Hippo—the one always used by *Good Day!* because it is a portable studio complete with two cameras and a switcher—was dispatched to the scene.

The switcher is of particular importance for *Good Day!* because the show depends a great deal on the Electronic Still Store (ESS), and only the switcher (man and machine) can bring what it holds in ready reserve to the screen. ESS is used in any number of ways in television, although most often as pictorial shots seen over the shoulder of whoever is speaking to illustrate and enliven what is being said. But in many cases ESS is used to fill the entire screen, as in the *Good Day!* logo or "billboard," a glass construction which the switcher causes to "fly in"—that is, to seem to come at the viewer from out of nowhere.

The script for this particular show thus begins: Cold open [Glenn Close] ten seconds; Billboard # ESS #1077 fly; host chat; Eileen [Prose] and Janet [co-hostess Langhart] welcome audience. During this one-minute "bite" the *Good Day!* music is played over the live applause and, it being a Friday, which is an audience-participation day, followed by tapes of scenes from *The Big Chill* and from the forthcoming *Maxie* with Janet's pretaped VOC (voice-over cassette). Then to ESS #1043—double boxes on a split screen with a shot of Janet in the studio and Cottle at the Four Seasons. And then finally—after a minute and forty seconds of elapsed time—to the actual seven-minute Glenn Close live remote interview.

Meanwhile another cassette has been readied with highlights from the life of Ruth Gordon, a good friend of Glenn Close's who had died shortly before. This would have been shown if Cottle had been able to steer the interview around to that subject. He was not, so that not inconsiderable effort was wasted.

Furthermore something apparently went wrong with Janet's taped voice-over, which ran longer than the scenes from *The Big Chill* and *Maxie* for reasons which were explained to me later but which I did not at the time grasp or for that matter even notice.

Then, at eight minutes and fifty seconds into the show, "Tom wraps, throws to Eileen," and the Glenn Close segment is finished. Actually as far as time goes it is only a half segment for all that effort involved.

Peggy Allen herself does most of the dealing with publishers. In May she went to San Francisco to attend the American Booksellers Association (ABA) convention (where publishers display their forthcoming books to book sellers) and, along with every other talk-show producer in the country and in competition with the two in her own market, made deals.

Carrying around her card catalogue with every author they had booked in the past year, she would approach, let us call them, Smithson and Hyde and, whipping out the pertinent card, announce, "We had seven S & H authors on our show last year, and we enjoyed all of them." ("They were blown away," she says.) Then she would continue, "Unlike our competition at *People Are Talking*, we do not usually do single-topic shows, but of course we can if the person warrants it. So if you will give me one of your big-shot authors I will promise to do some of your lesser people." (Having twice been on *Good Day!* myself in the latter capacity, I can't help wondering, now that I know the routine, which bigwig they were able to bag by being willing to take me.)

In a number of instances Allen makes tradeoffs with a publisher. A case in point involved losing Shirley MacLaine to *People Are Talking* in September in order to get Geraldine Ferraro for *Good Day!* in November. On the face of it the two seem to be about even as drawing cards, but the reason Peggy Allen chose Ferraro was that November, when she would be making the circuit to promote her book, is a "sweep" month, and to get the first woman candidate for vice-president in a sweep month was in Allen's view "a damn good deal."

Time-out here to explain that there are four sweep months a year—February, May, July, and November. At the end of each of these key months, sweep books are issued stating the Nielsen and Arbitron share and ratings plus the all important demographics for each of the 1,200 or so TV stations in every market in the country. These books are vital because they are the only guideline the television industry has for measuring how advertising rates should be set. (Newspapers, after all, have circulation figures with which to confront a potential advertiser.) Therefore, if McDonald's, say, wants to test its new McPickle 'n' Hamwich to see how it will play in Peoria and other assorted markets, they ask for the figures from the most recent sweeps book to determine where their spot advertising will be the most effective.

Needless to say, sweep months are not the time that Chet Curtis and Natalie Jacobson or any of the first-line talent choose to take a vacation. They *are* the time that the news programs put on their most compelling special segments, and that the two major locally produced programs, *Good Day!* and *Chronicle*, save their best material. But aside from such obvious best-foot-forward steps, things go on more or less as usual at WCVB.

Some stations, however, treat the sweep months with ludicrous intensity. I recall a time in February when I was vacationing in Southern California and Paul La Camera arranged for me to visit Los Angeles KABC-TV, an ABC "owned and operated" ("O and O" in the trade), just to compare how another station operated.

When I called to try to set up an appointment, my request was met with stunned disbelief. The program director's secretary insisted there must be some mistake. Surely Mr. La Camera had not realized that I was proposing to visit the station during *sweep* month, and surely he would understand that they could not possibly squeeze in even a half-hour of the program director's time for me during this critical period. (Mr. La Camera only laughed when he heard later of all this nonsense.)

However, I persisted. How about their public affairs person? Could he or she give me an hour or so? Even over the phone I could hear the secretary throw her hands in the air. The public affairs woman was up to her ears. Even worse to think she could see me during sweep month. Still I dared to ask the secretary if perhaps she herself could spare me a

Good Day!'s Joanne Tardieu and Rob Stegman with Eileen Prose

few minutes. Here her strained patience snapped altogether, and she told me in no uncertain terms that the station was off limits to all visitors during sweep months. If I would care to come back again in March, she would try to arrange to have me see someone who might help me.

I am glad to report that WCVB's more normal response to the November sweeps produced quite good results. *Chronicle* came up with a very respectable 10 rating and a 17 share in Nielsen, which consistently rates WCVB programs a bit higher than Arbitron, and *Good Day!* scored, again from Nielsen, a 5 rating and a 24 share, its highest numbers since February 1977. For this Joe Heston and Peggy Allen may take a bow, as should the two anchorwomen, Eileen Prose who has been with the show for eight years, and Janet Langhart, who started when *Good Day!* did

Good Day!'s Janet Langhart

but left television altogether for a number of years, then was lured back as an important draw when Joe Heston joined the station and started *Good Day!* on its upward spiral.

Having thus tossed bouquets, perhaps now is a good time to look in on a contrasting ceremony which is acted out each Friday by the *Good Day!* staff. It is called the Turkey of the Week Poll, and it is carried out by ten or so members of the staff plus the talent gathered in Peggy Allen's cramped, cluttered office in the basement and nether reaches of the Bennett Building. After the usual rehash of the day's show is completed, a large copper urn is passed around into which each person puts his or her vote for the worst, most embarrassing segment of the week. As I sat in on the meeting one day, the choices scribbled in my notes were, as nearly as I can read them some months later, Hair Coloring, Police Rape, Brooke Shields, two unreadable entries, and then the runaway favorite, Titanic.

In this segment, which I happened to watch at home,

Janet was supposed to interview an actual survivor from the 1912 disaster who was living in Woods Hole at the age of eighty-seven. To begin with, the old gentleman was understandably somewhat deaf, but even if he'd had the hearing of a twenty-year-old it wouldn't have improved matters. Something too technically complex to describe went wrong with the sound, and the survivor couldn't hear Janet's voice at all. So he just talked, and Janet was forced to pose her questions as generally as she could in the hope of making it seem as if what he had just said was in response to what she had just asked, which of course it wasn't.

As a matter of fact I have a few, hitherto unspoken, turkeys of my own that strengthen my impression that the show sometimes tries to out-Donahue Donahue in dealing with erotic subjects that they think will stimulate their stay-at-home audience of women.

For these episodes, which run oftener than I think they should, *Good Day!* has latched onto a sort of poor man's Ruth Westheimer, a sweet-looking, white-haired motherly soul, cast against type for her role as an anything-goes sex therapist.

I have in mind one particular segment, complete with studio audience and telephone calls, on the subject of "coupling," which is probably unnecessary for me to explain but I will anyway. It involves couples not only exchanging mates for sexual intercourse but actually standing by and watching as their husband or wife copulates, before it becomes their turn to change from voyeurs to participants.

The sex therapist was all in favor of this, to her, innocent pastime. She was also quick in answering some leading question to assure her audience that "no kinky sex" was practiced in these encounters. To which Janet Langhart—to her credit, I thought—noted dryly that some might possibly look upon coupling itself as rather kinky.

I agree, and suggest that such titillating quasi-erotic

Good Day!'s Director Mark Gentile and Assistant Program Producer Crystal Johns

segments, along with—even worse—the generally shallow, trivial tone of these daytime programs, pander to a sort of game-show, I-only-read-it-at-the-beauty-parlor mentality. Still, *Good Day!* and its local archrival, *People Are Talking*, aim a little higher than most of the equivalent shows seen in other parts of the country, notably in Los Angeles, where the emphasis seems to be almost exclusively on beauty aids.

But *Good Day!* and *People Are Talking* not only should be better but *could* be if they didn't keep such a wary eye on each other, each afraid to deviate too much from the mediocre norm for fear of giving a rating advantage to the other.

Both—in fact all such daytime shows—make the mistake,

which is television's fatal weakness anyway, of playing to the lowest rather than the highest common denominator. The results run counter to their professed concern with "quality programming."

12:00–12:30

While Isaac Laughinghouse is directing *Good Day!* from the control room and Peggy Allen is fretting, with restraint, about whatever her perfectionist's eye sees going wrong with her show, in the Newsroom behind them, the *Eyeopener* talent and producer Phil Levy, now in the sixth hour of their working day, are readying the *Midday News* . . . and finding this process something of an anomaly.

It could almost be said that the most notable thing about the *Midday News* is that it exists at all. Most stations, both in larger and certainly in smaller markets, pay little or no attention to news at this hour. Los Angeles, for example, has no news program at noon on any of its stations. In New York one can see news only on one out of seven stations, and in Chicago on one out of five. But in Boston all three commercial stations carry a twelve o'clock news program, and in this fiercely competitive market, what one station does in news the other two must pretty well do also.

In general, news tends to get rather short shrift at noon since midday is an awkward time for TV coverage (although far less so for radio). Most stories are in the process of *happening* at that hour but are not yet resolved. So, as Phil Levy, producer of the CVB *Midday*, observes, he has the option of running what he can get of a breaking but still not "wrapped" story and informing his audience that more on this will be forthcoming at six o'clock, or not running it at all and leaving it to six o'clock to give a beginning, a middle, and an ending—if ending there is by then—to the piece.

As an instance, not long ago the perpetrators of a much-

Isaac Laughinghouse in the control room

touted bank heist in suburban Medford were identified and apprehended after a long and baffling search. News of this breakthrough reached WCVB at around nine-thirty in the morning, and reporter Susan Wornick was dispatched to the local courthouse. Shortly before noon she called in to report that the three suspects had been arraigned but were not yet indicted and would not be until after the *Midday News* was off the air.

Levy, knowing this would be a big if not the lead story on the six o'clock news, still decided that he might as well take what he could get for the *Midday*. Accordingly, Susan Wornick appeared live, giving such information as she already had and throwing to Jim Boyd ("Back to you, Jim"). Better than nothing, Levy thought, and, since neither of the other stations chose the option of running such an incomplete spot, it counted as a sort of beat for Channel 5. Interestingly enough, Channels 4 and 7 wrapped the story on the following day, by which time it was yesterday's news to Phil Levy and not worth air time.

What *is* worth air time, then? Certainly not the previous day's 6:00 and 11:00 P.M. news, which is often repeated on the *Eyeopener*. Sometimes international stories can get important play because the time factor, at least in Europe, is in our favor.

But when the Nobel Peace Prize was given in Oslo to the International Physicians for the Prevention of Nuclear War, accompanied by vigorous and vivid protest against one of the Russian doctors who had made previous anti-Sakharov comments, it was 7:00 A.M. our time. Certainly there was plenty of time for a live shot on the *Midday*. However, to Levy's frustration ABC ran exactly nine seconds of video during their *Good Morning America*, which he could have had but found unacceptably brief, and Cable News's next satellite feed was not scheduled until 1:00 P.M., aiming of course for the six o'clocks. So what Levy did was order graphics for both the prize ceremony and the protest, and as Jim Boyd read forty seconds of copy, these appeared as effects (ESS) behind him.

"Most of the time," says Levy, "I actually have to lobby the assignment desk for stories I want. And it's tough because I know that if they have a choice of doing a live story that will only get on the air once that day, they'll automatically do it for the six o'clock and not for us."

I suggested that it seemed the *Midday* was treated rather like a stepchild.

"Your word!" he pounced. "I'm glad you said that so I didn't have to."

But then he added that the *Midday* was really more like radio—an interim show, an up-to-the-minute status report. And, he further noted, it has the distinction of being the

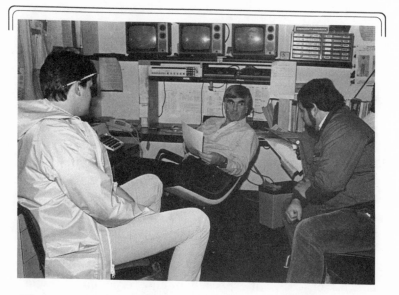
The news assignment desk

only news show which is for the most part written by the talent and in which they also play a major part in making decisions.

Accordingly Susan Burke, Jim Boyd, Levy, and sometimes an associate producer sit down at nine o'clock, after Susan and Jim have done their five-minute stints on *Good Morning America*, and figure out what should be on the *Midday* and how it should flow.

Flow (Levy's word), implying a smooth, uninterrupted, steady stream, hardly applies, however, to this program, which in point of fact has only *nine* minutes of actual news for its half-hour on the air.

When Levy pointed this out to me, I looked so doubtful that he gave me a breakdown as follows: 20 seconds to get on and 20 to get off; 1 minute, 20 seconds for teases; 6

minutes for three commercials; 1 minute, 45 seconds for the daily Mr. Food cooking segment, which includes 15 seconds for his sponsor; 3 minutes for weather; 3 minutes for sports. Neither of these features is actually counted, in Levy's mind at least, as straight news, nor is the 2-minute, 45-second "kicker" that usually winds up the show, consisting of some humorous piece by Chuck Kraemer, the resident wit, or by Paula Lyons, the house consumer expert, or some offbeat spot about sea lions frolicking in Florida waters.

Add this all up and be off the air by 12:28 to allow for a 1-minute, 30-second editorial, and you wind up with 9 minutes, 10 seconds of news divided into approximately ten or eleven stories.

Such is the tyranny of the clock in all television, whether network or local, but especially in news programs and most especially in the *Midday* news, which, as the hour of the day suggests, is neither quite here nor there.

There was one fateful exception, however, when the *Midday* played a vital role in the long-to-be-remembered disaster of the *Challenger* shuttle, which exploded seventy seconds into its flight, snuffing out the lives of the seven astronauts aboard.

The tragedy occurred on Tuesday, February 28, 1986, at 11:39 A.M. One of the astronauts to die was the much-heralded "first ordinary citizen in space," schoolteacher Christa McAuliffe. Because the ebullient thirty-seven-year-old Mrs. McAuliffe came from Concord, New Hampshire, which is in Channel 5's viewing area, the station had assigned reporter Shirley McNerney to cover the teacher at intervals from the moment she entered the program seven months earlier. As a matter of course, then, Shirley McNerney was standing by at Cape Canaveral with a live NewsStar truck and time booked on the satellite to cover the blast-off and crowd re-

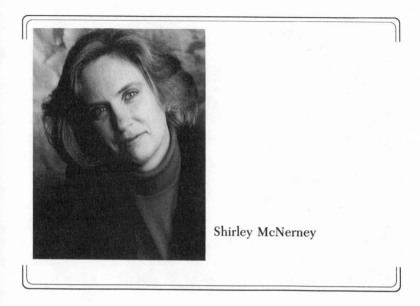

Shirley McNerney

action. This was to have been the lead story—for once a really big one—for the *Midday News*.

Interest in the flight, however, had pretty much flagged because there had been so many delays, the second-to-last one being on the Sunday that the New England Patriots were, for the first time in their history, playing in the Super Bowl. Such was the wild local excitement over this hyped-up sports drama that numerous people remembered say in passing on Super Bowl Sunday that they forgot to even watch to see if the "teacher had got into space."

Nonetheless, two days later when the lift-off did finally occur, many of the staff at WCVB and certainly most of the key news people were standing around watching Cable News Network (CNN) coverage of the actual event.

Emily Rooney, assistant news director, recalls that just as the orbiter started to rise off the launch pad, one of the reporters, David Ropeik, said, "For some reason this one makes me nervous. I guess because there's one of us ordinary

Master control

mortals on board." And at that instant the explosion happened.

At first no one reacted. Everyone, most notably the people watching live at Cape Canaveral, assumed that the burst of flame was simply the usual solid rocket burn we have all become so accustomed to seeing at lift-off. But then came the dreadful words from the Mission Control commentator: "Obviously a major malfunction."

The entire Newsroom swept into action. For just a second, though, they hesitated thinking they should put Jim Boyd, who was right there and ready to go on the *Midday News*, on camera to warn the viewers—"We interrupt this program to bring you . . . " But then they all decided that would waste too much vital time. What they needed to do was get those

Cable Network News pictures live from the Cape out fast for the public to see.

Fortunately Channel 5 is the only station in Boston that has a formal arrangement that gives them the right to carry CNN video and audio on their programs. So Phil Balboni gave the order to Master Control to cut off the currently running soap *Ryan's Hope* and punch up CNN. Within two and a half minutes of the explosion, WCVB was on the air with pictures from Cape Canaveral—the first station in town to be there.

After a long run of pictures, many of which we would see over and over and over again, Jim Boyd did come on and briefly orient the viewing audience to what was happening before they cut to ABC for a terse announcement of the tragedy from the White House. Peter Jennings had not yet arrived on the scene but was to get there momentarily. Steve Bell was carrying on for the network.

By this time the clock had moved up to, if not a little bit past, the normal start-up of the *Midday News*. Jim and Mary Ann Kane sitting in for Susan Burke, who was ill, went on camera cold, without any of the usual *Midday News* opening footage, which seemed superfluous because by then they were in contact with Shirley McNerney via satellite from the Cape.

Naturally everyone wanted desperately to hear what she had to say. They had previously booked satellite time for her for two minutes, so Emily Rooney had to call CONUS (Continental United States) in Minneapolis, which is the satellite consortium from which they lease, to try to get more time. She was amazed at how easily she was able to accomplish this, primarily, she assumes, because shuttle flights had seemed to most TV stations to be pretty routine by then and not many had booked time ahead. At any rate she was able to arrange to have Shirley on for two ten-minute bites, during which time Jim and Mary Ann simply interviewed her; they had no script, no prepared questions, no wire copy, nothing at all to guide them except their own instincts. "We just asked the questions we thought any regular member of the audience would want to know," Jim Boyd said later, "and Shirley was magnificent. I've never seen anybody better. She had poured herself into this story, but she was very composed and able to stop and be very professional."

Still, she was not so professional that she seemed coldly remote. "Shirley didn't de-emotionalize herself," says Emily Rooney. And in fact, although her voice was steady and she answered each question as fully as she could, she looked devastated. She had, after all, known Christa McAuliffe well. "I feel just terrible about this," she said at one point. And you knew she truly did.

By the time she had finished her stints, Dr. Michael Guillen, WCVB's science editor, had arrived, so Jim and Mary Ann interviewed him for about fifteen minutes before going off the air locally at 12:45, one hour after they had gone on.

"I was up there professionally," says Jim, "but I really didn't want to be there. I wanted to be a human being and vent my sorrow. But I couldn't do that until I got home."

Producer Phil Levy doubtless did the same thing when he got home, but in the event this kind man who is often frustrated in his job, had the time of his life being in the center of the excitement, and, not realizing how it might have sounded, exulted, "It was a ball."

That surely it was not, but still it was an eminently coverable TV story. "TV elevates what it touches," wrote Bob Kuttner in the *Boston Globe*. "If TV's heroes are larger than life, then their deaths must be made larger too." He was not the first nor the last to sound off against the TV hype on this tragic occasion.

Critic Jeff Greenberg expressed a slightly different view a few days later. "TV was a national gathering place for us on that terrible day," he said, and might indeed have added that TV performed that rite with distinction.

5

Role Models

THE SOAPS ARE ON NOW. Only one man in master control is pushing the buttons that bring *Loving*, *All My Children*, *One Life to Live*, and *General Hospital* from the affiliate network to the home screens.

This, then, seems a good stretch of the broadcast day to look behind the silent cameras at Channel 5 and see what various key people are doing. Key young people for the most part, role models for the hoards of even younger hopefuls who dream of somehow making themselves a part one day of this wondrous, ever-changing television scene.

Richard Dickinson, thirty-seven, is WCVB's art director, a title he considers a slight misnomer; he prefers to think of himself as head of the graphic design department. "I would probably not hire an illustrator who came and asked me for a job," he says, and when I look puzzled, he explains, "I must have designers who can *manipulate* information into visual treatment. I need people who can cope with the electronic computer age we are now in in television, who understand the vast terminology. Good graphic designers are almost always enhancing other people's ideas, not editorializing their own, whereas illustrators are closer to fine arts, so they become involved with promoting a message that is their own. And in this business that can become the wrong message."

Dickinson, a graduate of the Rhode Island School of Design, participated heavily during the late sixties in protesting the Vietnam War. His involvement with that turbulent period has left its mark. He is a man of contradictions, often cynical, for example, about television, which he says he is pretty sure he doesn't really like. He knows, however, that his primary love is good design, and he is extremely proud of a staff that has won five Emmys in a row for its work. "I expect everyone that I hire to be able to design a nice book, a good brochure, a handsome living area, an exciting event," he says, "and I don't think we would have won those Emmys if I hadn't promoted the positive aspects of good, thinking designers."

Paradoxically, the reason he is wary of TV is that he believes there are actually *too many* of the graphic effects he spends his life creating, and not enough content. "I think it's fine to have all the gimmicks, but because they're there doesn't mean you have to use them all the time. For people that watch television it's like having goulash every night for supper. But I think, with all due respect, that's what the viewing audience wants. I mean, if you're going to entice someone to watch, they've got to be razzle-dazzled."

And indeed the gimmicks are awesome in sophistication and complexity, and frustrating to write about since they are continually identified only by letters (often no one is sure what they stand for) or words that are not yet in any dictionary.

Prime among the visual-effects creators, however, is a

computer whose simple, direct name belies its intricacy. It is called the Paint Box, and it produces all the still images that have long since replaced old-fashioned slides. The Paint Box itself can be mastered by a graphic artist in three or four weeks, says Dickinson. And actually it looks quite straightforward. A 2 1/2-by-3-foot "tablet" on which the artist "wipes" (draws) is made of white Formica, overlaying the electronic circuitry. What is wiped by the artist shows not on the tablet but on the screen in front of it. The various commands and modes seem familiar enough to anyone who have ever used a word processor, although obviously what emerges on the screen is very, very different.

"The Paint Box can do anything," says Dickinson, "along with the DVE [there we go again—Digital Visual Effects], which manipulates the image. It can expand or reduce, give a high metallic look, imitate airbrushing, chalk drawings, watercolor, anything an artist needs to provide a visual effect. It can also copy photographs, change the backgrounds, add shadows, change the nose on the subject; it can draw pictures, cartoons, add letters. It can make whatever is being created full-screen or infinitesimal; it can elongate a square, make it a circle, squash it down. Although it has what Dickinson refers to as "limited animation capability"—it can make an eye blink, for instance—it cannot move whole figures or objects by itself. That requires a switcher.

Both the Paint Box and the DVE are made by a British company called Quantel (other companies also make this equipment), so there is a tendency at Channel 5 to refer to the manipulated images as Quantels.

I have witnessed Paint Box images being made of Bernard Cardinal Law, much embellished from a photograph at the time of his investiture in Rome; of a giraffe for reasons I don't remember; and of a Patriot reaching out to grab a pass at the time the New England team won the AFC championship in Miami. These images, (possibly with the exception of the giraffe) will be numbered and filed in the Electronic Still Storer (ESS).

Dickinson feels impelled to keep reminding me that "what most people don't realize about this department is that none of our things move without the orchestration of the switching person, the director, the assistant director, and the audio man in the control room. It is a cast of thousands, and since we have gone electronic a lot of coordination is needed both in mind and spirit. Let's face it, if you are a very egotistical prima donna, you'll have a hell of a time dealing with six or seven people to produce a show opening, let alone one that ever gets completed to your satisfaction."

The biggest challenge facing Dickinson recently was to help in the creation of an entirely new opening to introduce all four of the daily news shows. It took three months to achieve this end, and Dickinson gives the whole credit to his art director for news, Warren Zucker. "My design just didn't feel right," he concedes, "but Warren came up with the winning solution. A big transparency—a huge slide, really, of the Boston skyline striated with vertical lines of varying widths."

To set this into place the entire studio had to be redone, and instead of the five-seated cloverleaf table in the middle of the studio area, a longer, wavy four-seated anchor desk has been placed on one side of the stage illuminated with red neon lights at the bottom. Behind this a large new Chromakey screen has been installed. (Readers may recall the green Chromakey screen in front of which the weathermen stand and pretend to be pointing at the Mississippi River when in fact they are pointing only to a blank screen [although viewers see the entire U.S. map on it] while reading from a map displayed on the teleprompter at the end of the camera.)

"On the news set," says Dickinson, "we now have a larger Chromakey, and the transparency of the skyline there is covered with gauze, like a scrim in the theater. So when light is turned on at the back of the transparency, you see the Boston skyline, and when you light the front or gauze side of the transparency, you see (in the studio) only the green electronic Chromakey surface, which can take any sort of video image, Paint Box, still, or tapes.

"For example, say Chief Correspondent Martha Bradlee has been sent to Washington to interview Tip O'Neill about young Joseph Kennedy's successful bid to win the speaker's about-to-be-vacated seat in the House of Representatives. And say the producer of the six o'clock news wants a shot of the Capitol for background. Well," says Dickinson, "if you want the talent in a local setting like Washington, you turn the light back to Chromo and lose the Boston skyline. Up comes your green color, and then you put in an effect of Washington and then over that you DVE a video effect with Quantel of Joe Kennedy squeezed down in a Paint Box image over Martha's shoulder."

Seeing me look rather frazzled by all this, Dickinson laughed. "When it comes to more and more effects," he told me, "I can talk you blue in the face."

Opting for the obvious, I said, "You have."

So he moved to some refreshingly nonelectronic aspects of his work and his department.

After he graduated from the Rhode Island School of Design in 1971, Richard Dickinson worked for an architectural firm in Boston, designing brochures, until after two years his job became redundant. He had made a good format for their brochures, which they could use over and over again. No use keeping him on the staff. He freelanced at other architectural firms for a while and then heard of an opening as assistant art director at Channel 5. He applied and was hired by Bob Bennett, staying on until 1978 when, as he says, "I became antsy and wanted to run my own department."

The opportunity to do just that arose at the CBS affiliate

in Washington, D.C., and he leaped at the chance. But after only eight months Bennett called him to say that the art director at Channel 5 had just left and did he want the job. He hesitated. He had been at the Washington station such a short time and was leery of getting the reputation as a drifter. More than that, he liked Washington and especially the news programs, which, he says, "make you understand *why* certain issues take the route they do. There you hear what is really happening and why. Up here in Boston you only know what is happening. You rarely know why."

But in the end, he says, "I really love this place and, apart from news, Washington didn't begin to do the quality of work they do here." None of the experimentation, the specials. Nothing like the current public-service campaign called *A World of Difference*, which dramatizes in a wide variety of spots the insidious evils of prejudice.* Dickinson thinks this is a great and useful program and had a great deal to do with promoting it by running a poster contest for public school students from grades one to twelve to make drawings illustrating the message. Twelve winners have had their work reproduced in the station's 1986 calendar—designed, of course, by the graphics department—and the winner of winners, a third-grader, had her enchanting drawing used as the station's Christmas card.

The department is responsible for all promotional material coming from WCVB, all sales sheets—they have a large type-setting machine squeezed in one corner of the supply room—all advertisements, billboards, subway cards, newspaper and *TV Guide* advertisements, printed, photographed, and designed, amounting to about thirty pieces a week.

Two staff photographers produce all the shots of the talent that adorns the walls outside the newsroom. These are de-

---

*Produced in conjunction with the Anti-Defamation League of B'nai B'rith, the Greater Boston Civil Rights Coalition, and the Shawmut Banks.

veloped in a darkroom that cannot be heated, a hazard which is characteristic of the inadequate space allotted to this most vital department. The staff is triumphant because, for the first time in their existence, they who deal in light and air have had a single window installed.

In fact, compared with the elegant executive offices, installed by Metromedia on the second floor of the building, the graphics people are housed like peasants—"Let them eat cake."

But no matter. They are at home in their mole hole; the noise and the cheer are manifest. "Everyone here is an artist, and they love what they do," says their boss.

When Martha Bradlee, Channel 5's chief correspondent, covered a mammoth Walter Mondale rally in Boston just before the presidential election in 1984, a gathering complete with all of Massachusetts's big political names, including Kennedy and O'Neill, she managed to wedge herself and her cameraman in with the network pool camera directly above Mondale. Since she was the only local reporter to achieve this most favored position, others covering the story looked at her with a decidedly jaundiced eye. One from a rival station fumed so vociferously about her tactics to his boss that his news director called Phil Balboni to complain about Martha's pushing and shoving.

Balboni, tongue in cheek, approached her. "Martha, were you pushing and shoving people around at the rally yesterday?"

"Phil," Martha replied, "I have to tell you that I haven't any idea. I only know I do whatever I did almost every day because I consider it part of my job."

If such is stereotypical TV reporter behavior, however, this slight, soft-spoken, engaging thirty-three-year-old woman does not fit the mold in other particulars. "I don't have TV looks," she says. "I don't have typical TV presence.

I'm serious and I work very hard. I want to find out as much as I can about every story I do. Any fool can go out and grab enough to fill two minutes and then leave. But believe me, it's not just what they say in those two minutes that counts. You have to work the phones, work sources, I think the challenge of TV is the gathering of an enormous amount of news and then condensing it into two minutes. That's where the talent comes. It's gritty. You're sort of like street fighters. And I love it. It suits me.

"Television reporting has an extra dimension for me; it has the wonderful visual aspect that newspaper reporting doesn't have. But of course newspaper reporters have advantages that we don't in length, time, and depth."

Martha Bradlee is able to compare the two media worlds pretty much at first hand since her husband, Ben, descendant of an old Boston family, is a prominent reporter for the *Boston Globe* and his father is the famed editor of the *Washington Post.*

She herself comes from Salt Lake City. She was in her last year at the University of Utah and floundering, hopping from one major and avocation to another, when she got her first job in a television station where her mother had once worked. In the finest television tradition, she started at the bottom doing what she calls shlock work, but meanwhile learning how to do everything—shoot film, do research, write and edit her own stuff. "And I thought, 'This is great. This really suits me.' You're always finding out new things and always changing. In this business it's important to know a little bit about a lot—or better still, a lot about a lot."

After two years she got a job as a general reporter at a better station in Salt Lake City, which is about the forty-fifth market in the country, and considered a very good one. So when she married, moved to Boston, and applied for a job at WCVB, she had good credentials and a tape that showed she could handle a wide variety of stories well. In

Richard L. Dickinson,
Vice President/Design Director

Martha Bradlee,
Chief Correspondent

1979 she was hired by Jim Thistle, Phil Balboni's predecessor, again as a general reporter.

She had been at WCVB for just a little over a year when she won an Emmy for spot reporting. The story, a heartwrencher, concerned a little autistic boy who had disappeared into the hills of New Hampshire while on a camping trip with his parents. Martha and her cameraman first arrived in New Hampshire after the boy had been missing for three days and did a quick piece for the eleven o'clock news. This story was heard by a Boston firefighter, himself the father of an autistic child, who immediately got into his car and drove through the night to New Hampshire and ultimately found the boy.

Martha and the cameraman arrived again on the scene just as the firefighter first handed the little boy over to his par-

ents. "I ended up saying about three words," Martha says.
"It was so moving, I just let the pictures tell the story." She
did interview the boy, but very briefly. Leaning over this
autistic child who was lying down staring at a butterfly he
had poised on his finger, she asked, "Were you frightened?"

"Frightened," was all he could or in fact needed to say.
Without a doubt she handled the story with taste and skill,
and after that she was pretty much a marked—in the best
sense—woman.

"Network quality," says Emily Rooney, assistant news director and Martha's immediate boss. "Even before that
Emmy, we knew she was network quality."

So did Channel 7, the CBS station, struggling to catch up
with the other two local stations. They offered her over twice
as much as she was making at Channel 5 to join them.

"I thought, gee, with that amount of money, I have to
take it," she explained. "Then I thought, no, I don't either.
I like it here. I feel very loyal to CVB. I'm happy in this
environment."

I questioned her about this loyalty to CVB (people in the
trade never bother to use the W), which seems to affect
everyone who works at this station. Is it genuine?

"Yes, it really is. This place is so different, cut from a
different mold from most stations. It's a special atmosphere,
it's caring, it's personal feeling for people. It's a lot of things
mixed up [and perhaps a pinch of Bob Bennett's "magic
dust"] that makes it so special."

So in the end Martha Bradlee turned down Channel 7.
But by a quirk of fate and one which caused Phil Balboni
great chagrin, then chief correspondent Joe Day, who had
also been offered a far larger salary at Channel 7, succumbed
to their lure.

The post of chief correspondent was briefly filled by someone else and then was open again. Martha Bradlee swears
she thought it was going to remain that way. She did not

know it was up for grabs. She insists that when Phil Balboni invited her to dinner she had no idea that he was doing so to offer her, at the age of twenty-nine, the chief correspondent job.

Not surprisingly there were rumors and stories in the press about how she lobbied for the job and even played hardball newsroom politics to get it. Martha denies this, and Balboni, she says, corroborates her denial.

And how did her colleagues respond?

She hesitates, choosing her words carefully. "In general terms I think they're supportive. I think my colleagues respect me, and I respect them. I also know that in a situation like this some people might get a little tense. But actually when I was named chief correspondent most of them went out of their way to tell me, 'Well, I may have wanted that job myself, but anyway I'm glad for you that you got it.' "

The chief correspondent is the person whom the station has designated as its number-one reporter. Having this position means that by definition Martha Bradlee gets most of the best, most challenging, and often late-breaking stories, usually of national or international importance. She frequently reports from Washington; she has traveled to Ethiopia, to Manila, has spent time in the Middle East at the height of the terrorist airplane hijacking scare. She has all the qualifications of a star reporter; she is gutsy, adventurous, resourceful, bright, and audacious.

Certainly being chief correspondent (and always so identified) has added greater stress and responsibility to Martha's professional life. Sent to Geneva to cover the first Reagan-Gorbachev meeting, she says she panicked. "Here I was up against people who deal with Reagan every day. They have Soviet experts at their fingertips, and I've got to go over there and be very prepared. I went to seminars at Harvard, I read constantly, everything I could get hold of. I read all the way over on the plane. I couldn't sleep at night. And when someone from here said to me, 'Hey, what are you worrying about? It's going to be great, it will be a party,' I thought, maybe I'm doing this all wrong. But I still don't think it's going to be any party for me. It's going to be pure strain and pure work. Which it was. But certainly very rewarding."

Inevitably her wide-ranging successes brought her to the attention of a network. In the summer of 1985 when her contract with Channel 5 was up for renewal, she was called to New York to audition, initially for CBS's program *Nightwatch*, which runs in the small hours, but ultimately to be worked in as a regular network correspondent.

"The audition went really well," she says, "but I think sometimes people are fooling themselves if they think they can have family and everything they want in their careers without sacrificing something. Women make the mistake of imagining they can do it all. But I honestly didn't believe I could be a national correspondent right now and have a satisfactory relationship with my daughter."

Since her husband is away much of the time on assignment for the *Globe*, the responsibility for their five-year-old daughter, Greta, rests very largely with Martha. "We get on wonderfully," she says. "And I'm proud of myself because I feel as if I've struck a balance between my child and my job."

And besides, she says, the more she thought about the national thing, the more she thought, "What's the difference? Why should it be so important to be on TV across the country? I travel enough as it is. At CBS I could be away for eight months. I could go through three months when I wouldn't be on the air at all, or I could end up working like crazy on a story that would be killed at the last minute or be cut to thirty seconds. And furthermore you lose editorial control. In fact," she added after a moment, "you lose control, period."

And yet she now has a network clause in her contract which permits her once each year to decide that she's leaving to go to the network. "Perhaps one day" she says. "Perhaps when Greta is eight or nine, it might be possible."

But, as will be seen later in these pages, the situation between local and network news is in a state of flux. The outcome may well be that people like Martha Bradlee—top reporters throughout the country—will have greater scope and a stronger voice working for a local station than for one of the networks.

Meanwhile a change in Martha's schedule has made her even more indispensable. At CVB the powers that be, obviously feeling that the chief correspondent's abilities should not be showcased on only one news program, have arranged that she should report on both the six and eleven o'clock news, which means that except on rare occasions she covers two different stories each day.

So instead of coming to work at ten and going out shortly thereafter to prepare her story for the six o'clock, she comes in at three in the afternoon, by which time there is waiting for her some major story to be researched and written in three hours. That finished, she gets her assignment for the eleven o'clock, which she works up and reports from the anchor desk.

My first thought on hearing of this change is that Martha, who is such an activist, on-the-scene reporter, would hate this new arrangement, which keeps her more at her desk and less on the streets.

But, as she points out, "The change was not made without consulting me, and on the whole I like it very much." Although she will be concentrating largely on national and international stories, she will still go out on the local political stories which are her forte.

And what about the hours? "Much better from the point of view of my time with my daughter," she says. "I'm there when she gets home from kindergarten, and I have three uninterrupted hours with her before I have to got to work. So I like it.

"Nobody is climbing up my ladder. I'll admit that sometimes I'm screaming and ranting to myself after a particularly frustrating day. But then always I stop and think that I have the greatest job in the world. I know how lucky I am to have fallen into something like this. It just suits me."

That is a phrase she uses a lot: "It just suits me." It has a pleasantly old-fashioned ring to it, curiously incongruous in this frenetic arena in which chief correspondent Martha Bradlee operates so effectively.

Every person discussed so far *spends* the station's money, often in large doses. But Deborah Sinay has the responsibility of bringing *in* the revenue, and generating the financial wherewithal that makes Channel 5 operate, and indeed operate at the huge profit it does. She assumed this obligation at the age of twenty-nine when she became the youngest vice-president and the first woman vice-president ever in the life of WCVB.

In my early exploratory visits to the station, Debbie Sinay's name was invoked over and over again. "Debbie can sell ten thirties [ten thirty-second commercial spots in an hour's program]. . . . Debbie has them lined up for the six o'clock news. . . . Debbie has a wonderful enthusiasm for selling the specials that we do. . . . You must ask Debbie about that. . . . "

So when finally I was able to catch her off the run and sit down to talk to her, I said, "It seems you are the fountainhead from which all the money flows."

And this pretty, slim, warm, vivacious young woman now in her thirties and pregnant with her first child did not deny it. "I would say so, yes," she answered, without false modesty.

I said, "In order to dramatize your role, I need to visualize

Debbie Sinay,
Vice President/Sales

you in action for the lead." And Debbie Sinay, who for all her vast influence has never been a reporter and therefore mistook my meaning of the word *lead* said, "But, I lead all the time. That's my job. I oversee a staff of twenty-seven people here at the station. I deal with our media buyers, I meet with our major advertisers, I talk constantly with Katz, our rep company, about syndication, and I also make decisions every day on what will or won't bring in revenue. Jim Coppersmith will call and ask me, 'Deb, how much money can we make on that program?' He must ask that three hundred times a week, and I then have to evaluate. Is it topical? Is it informational? Will it get great ratings? And if I can come up with positives to these, then we start to negotiate, which means Paul La Camera and Jim will come to me and say, 'How much can we charge?' So that's where the numbers-crunching comes in."

I need to know specifics. What can they charge, say, for a spot in Prime Time?"

She tells me that the average Prime Time thirty-second

spot runs between $4,000 and $5,000. The high would be *Dynasty* at $8,000 or $9,000.

"And in Daytime?" I ask.

She considers. "Phil Donahue would be a pretty good example." Then reconsiders. "But first I want to be sure you understand exactly what happens in program sales." Which is just her nice way of saying she is sure I don't understand. So she explains.

"ABC, our affiliate network, pays us a nominal fee—and I mean nominal, $200 to $220 an hour—to carry their programs, and we can then go out and sell our own spots, a certain number of them, for whatever the market will bear. Then besides that, there are three ways of selling a program.

"The first is that the station pays cash, which means that we own the entire program. In other words the syndicator comes to Jim Coppersmith and Paul La Camera and says, 'I want you to buy this program, and I want you to pay cash.' That means that we own every spot and every break and can get revenue from every position.

"The second way is diametrically opposed. In the second way the syndicator *gives* us the program, and in turn they take some of the commercial breaks for barter. Let's say we had an hour program in prime time. The standard would be five two-minute breaks, which comes to twenty thirty-second spots. So if it was barter, they would give us ten thirties to sell locally and they, the syndicator, would take the other ten.

"Now, the third way of doing it is cash and barter. In that case we pay a small fee and take more spots. Instead of splitting it fifty-fifty, we would split it, say, thirty-seventy, with us taking the seventy. Meaning they get six spots and we get fourteen. And that's the way we do *Donahue*."

"But then you have to figure out how much to charge for your spots?"

"Exactly. Say Phil Donahue is charging a thousand dollars for his spots. We have to try to come up to that or even better if we can. So our figure is based on rating, share, on what the market will bear in Daytime for the number-one show in the morning, bar none, which means it's a demand area. That is people really want to be associated with it."

"And if they don't particularly want to be associated?"

"Then we have to entice them."

Here, of course, is where the artistry in all forms of selling comes into play. Only in the case of selling TV spots, Sinay and her colleagues are often dealing with an amorphous product whose virtues have to be taken on faith. The locally produced specials for which the station has long been famous fall into this category.

Looking back a few years, Sinay recalls a program CVB did called *Our Town Revisited*, a new look at the town of Peterborough, New Hampshire, which had been the inspiration for Thornton Wilder's 1938 play *Our Town*. The idea was to see how, in the years that had passed, life in this quiet hamlet compared with the fictional life portrayed by Wilder. A fanciful idea, charming and wistful, but not on the face of it the stuff to attract Toyota trucks, Midas Mufflers, Coca-Cola bottling plants, or McDonald's.

But Debbie Sinay has two inherent qualities which enabled her to sell *Our Town Revisited* to this very sort of company: optimism and enthusiasm, plus one acquired capability—know-how.

"I think what's great about this station," she says, "is that it has such a wonderful reputation that when I go knocking on a door and say, 'Hi, I'm Debbie Sinay from WCVB,' I am immediately welcomed. And with *Our Town Revisited*, because it was a local story, locally produced, people wanted to be a part of it."

"In theory perhaps, but how did you actually describe it in selling terms?"

"We spent time with people in research putting together what we call a salable one sheet that we could take to the marketplace and show buyers just the heart of what we were doing with the program, plus tempting little snippets from scenes already shot. We don't talk dollars and cents on the one sheet. That comes later when the salespeople who are trained to sell numbers follow up with pricing the show competitively."

"But you obviously don't know the numbers before the show runs."

"No, we have to sell it based on our predictions, which in turn are based on past performances. Actually *Our Town Revisited* was very easy to sell, just as long as we were given enough time to do it."

Shifting ground, we consider another, much trickier kind of special, one for which Sinay knows there is bound to be a certain buyer resistance. As an example she cites a recent special, *Gays in Boston*, which she calls a classic case in point.

"When the program people came to me and said, 'We want to do a homosexual special. Is it salable?,' I said no. But if it is something important that we really want to do, then profit is not the issue."

So they did it. Knowing that they would have limited advertisers and that in the normal half-hour show there would be twelve thirty-second spots, what Sinay did was "cut the show" differently so that there would be only six thirties instead of twelve.

"And what did you do with the extra time?"

"Put it back into the program itself, and sold the six thirties."

Compelling specials like these, plus the newscasts and

Chronicle, are what General Manager Coppersmith refers to as the champagne in the freezer and the foie gras in the pantry. "But," he adds, "there's got to be some place for the bread and butter too."

"That vast wasteland which is television," Newton Minow once termed it, and it seems he must have had in mind that bread-and-butter period, those hours devoted not to news nor to local programming nor to network specials, but the humdrum hours, intellectually speaking, of the broadcast day. For all these times Debbie Sinay must and does find sponsors, often more readily than in the more stimulating offerings.

We consider the Day Part called early fringe, which covers the hours from 4:00 to 6:00 P.M.: reruns of *Dynasty*, 4:00 to 5:00, followed by a half-hour of *Too Close for Comfort*, a sitcom owned by WCVB, and then the perennial *All in the Family* from 5:30 to 6.

Seeing my pained look, Debbie Sinay laughs. "Those may not be the kinds of shows you would want to see, but believe me, there is a market out there for them."

"But surely Archie Bunker is over the hill by now," I protest.

"Archie Bunker is an interesting case. That show has run on our air longer than it ran on the networks. In fact, it is one of the longest-running off-network shows in the history of television. We've had it on . . . it's got to be nine years."

"All the more reason to replace it with something fresh," I suggest.

"Hey," says Sinay cheerfully, "it's a lot better than game shows."

"That it is."

"And this station never does game shows. Never. And Archie Bunker does very well, even against *Wheel of Fortune* on Channel 7, which is the all-time top-rated game show. It doesn't win the time period, but it holds its own." And she shows me the huge fat rating book based on the sweep months to prove it. *All in the Family* gets an 8 rating and a 20 share against *Wheel of Fortune*'s 10 and 24.

"This is our bible," she says as I stare boggle-eyed at rows and rows of microscopic figures in column after column of abbreviated headings. "These are the demographics. So, staying with Archie Bunker as long as we're there already, you'll see that among women aged eighteen to forty-nine it gets an 81, which means eighty-one thousand, as opposed to *Wheel*'s 51. Among the same-aged men it gets 49 to *Wheel*'s 46, among teens it gets a 12 to *Wheel*'s 22, and among children two to eleven, 27 to 30."

She looks at me, amused.

"It's sort of intriguing," I say, surprised that I mean it.

To Debbie Sinay it is endlessly intriguing, challenging, and exciting. She came to her fascination with sales working at the other end of the spectrum as a media buyer for Boston's venerable department store, Jordan Marsh.

Born in Norwich, Connecticut, she took her college degree in education (not communication) at Boston University and worked summers in a radio station in her hometown. After graduation she first took a job as a secretary, there being no other openings in the early seventies for women with her qualifications, but then she moved on to Jordan Marsh, where she remained for five and a half years before moving over to Channel 5 in the BBI days. She was and is a great admirer of Leo Beranek, who gave her her chance and then made her a vice-president, and who holds her in high regard as one of the most enterprising people he helped bring into the BBI fold.

She is married to Charlie Kravetz, who was one of the creators of *Chronicle* and, until his move to the news department, its executive producer. It is a program his wife sells with special enthusiasm and success ("People stand in line to sponsor it"), not only because it is her husband's, she insists, but because it is "a public affairs program that deals forthrightly with issues, with people and the quality of their lives."

In a way *Chronicle* is the essence of what WCVB stands for. And by the same token, so is Debbie Sinay.

6

Newstime: 6:00 to 7:00 P.M.

NewsCenter 5 at six! Linchpin of the entire day, top revenue producer of local programming, culmination of the work of the "talent"— twelve general reporters assigned to this program, six male and six female, and, most salient, showcase for the highly rated, popular anchor team of Natalie Jacobson and Chet Curtis, along with the two other first-string members, sportscaster Mike Lynch and weatherman Dick Albert.

The importance of anchorpersons cannot be overstated. In the view of many, news programs are primarily reflections of an anchor team, most often a man and a woman, who are the conduit—the messengers, if you will—who bring the news, usually more bad news than good.

Without question, most viewers decide which six o'clock newscast they are going to watch on the basis of whether or not they like, identify with, and trust the anchors and, to a lesser but still notable degree, the sportcaster and weatherman.

"Natalie is a major star," says Phil Balboni, and adds, "A lot of what's right about this business is Chet and Natalie. They're intelligent and thoughtful and they care." There is also, he might have added, an intriguing personal dimension since they are married and have a little girl, so are in fact a real family.

Ironically Jacobson is a name Natalie would rather not be using, since it belongs to her former husband. And because she is very proud of her Serbian heritage, she would have preferred to use her maiden name, Salatich, or if not that, then her married name, Curtis. However, Leo Beranek, back in the BBI days when this anchor team evolved, did not want a Curtis and Curtis. The alternative, Chet points out, would have been for him to take back his original Polish name of Kukiewicz; Salatich and Kukiewicz, Chet muses would have been quite a combination. Not unreasonably the BBI chiefs settled for Jacobson and Curtis.

But for quite a while before they had to come to that decision, Natalie was the bigger talent, already entrenched anchoring the six and eleven o'clock news. In fact, while Chet was still laboring, first on the *Eyeopener-Midday* shift and then on the weekend news, Natalie was being wooed by CBS.

"I was offered a lot both in terms of money and position," she says. "God knows where I got the good sense to turn that down, but I'm glad I did. Of course, it was a tremendous ego boost. The president of CBS calling me to New York a couple of times, saying 'Why don't you want to come and work for me?' But I now know that my decision was right. I didn't feel I was ready to do some of those network jobs, and also I thought I could be more effective as a local reporter. I like the give and take we have on the local scene."

Natalie's co-anchor on this local scene then was a smooth article named Tom Ellis, whom people either loved or disliked intensely. Natalie, professional that she is, appeared not to let her feelings about him show, but the fact was, according to Balboni, that Ellis made her mad, which made her competitive, which in the view of some made her a better anchor. But after the earlier-mentioned visit by the Queen of England, the chemistry between Chet and Natalie was so good (by then both on and off the air) that it was decided to inject Chet into the evening news mix, a troika that Chet thinks never worked.

Fortunately it came to an end quite abruptly when Ellis, without prior notice, cleaned out his locker, as it were, left a note under Bob Bennett's door, and departed for the richer pay dirt at Channel 7 (from which he has since been fired).

In talking to TV news talent, one soon observes how few of them have had any experience in the so-called print medium. There seems to be no logical progression anymore from newspaper reporters to television reporters (or directors or producers either, for that matter). Chet and Natalie are cases in point.

Chet started his career at the age of twelve in Schenectady, New York, singing on a TV program called *Teen-Aged Barn*. He then got a job as a "gofer" at a local radio station, and progressed to a regular program interviewing kids from four to five in the afternoon, which he maintained until he went on to Ithaca College in 1956. While there studying for a communications degree, he started working at the commercial radio station and after graduation moved on to work at a Rochester, New York, television station, where he remained for three years. Then in 1963 he went to WTOP in Washington, D.C., where he spent another three years, then to WCBS, New York, and finally to WHDH, Boston, in 1968.

Natalie greatly regrets that she had no newspaper experience and still stands somewhat in awe of that branch of the profession. "When I first started in television," she says, "and a news conference closed, I always waited for the print

Charlie Kravetz, Senior Executive Producer, and
NewsCenter 5's Natalie Jacobson

journalist to close with 'Thank you, Mr. President,' or 'Mr. Whatever.' " Nowadays the senior television person, who is usually Natalie, performs this honor, but even so, she says, "If there's an older print journalist there, I'll still wait for him or her out of courtesy."

She was born in Chicago but has lived most of her life in the East, going to the University of New Hampshire. After a couple of years in business, she started at Channel 56, one of the UHF stations in Boston, then still struggling. In fact she had only been there six months when their entire news operation folded, so she moved on to Channel 4, where she remained for two and a half years, working in public affairs but at the same time learning, she says, a tremendous amount about broadcasting.

Chet Curtis with Linda Polach

"This is a fast business," she says. "I would never make it as a researcher, for example, and have to wait to see the results of my labors ten years down the road. I think I would even have trouble now in working for a magazine, where it would drive me crazy waiting for my stuff to be printed, whereas in TV your story is right there in living color. It's either good or it isn't. But the negative side is that unlike a newspaper, you can't turn the page back and read a story again. You have just one shot."

As far as being an anchor is concerned, she feels that most people imagine the anchors have a great deal more authority than they do, that they pass on every story and how it is to be presented ("live or just pop a reporter in the field to wrap around his or her tape"). The fact is, however, that there is hardly a day when Natalie and Chet do not disagree with some part of their two programs. "And," she adds, "that's how it should be."

Boston's three VHF stations, but more particularly WBZ and WCVB, have for a number of years run neck and neck in the ratings, but then unhappily there came a time when Balboni saw his six and eleven o'clock newscasts sliding quite definitely into second place. "This was a terrible psychological blow," he said. "The ratings told us that our trend line was downward, that the viewers' preference was away from us."

To arrest this slide, Balboni began instituting a series of brainstorming sessions with the four members of his anchor team in which they frankly looked at their performances as a group and discussed how they were relating to each other and how they could do better in their jobs. "I think these meetings were very positive," he says, "and helped to foster a good spirit in difficult times."

I was doubtful. I told Balboni I couldn't just write that they had these meetings and determined to do better. Was the problem with their journalistic skills, with the objectivity of their presentation, the accuracy of their facts? No, it seemed none of these factors was in question. But, unlike any other disseminators of news or information, television anchors must have that special indefineable quality that gives them influence or authority over large numbers of people. They must have charisma.

"The core of it," said Balboni "was the perception we all came to that some of our newscasts lacked sparkle and energy and a sense of excitement. To a large degree these are qualities that *must* be communicated by the anchors. So what we had to find out was why there wasn't more of a sense of urgency. Why was it that they weren't able to project a sense of enjoyment in their jobs and make the viewers feel comfortable and at ease?

"Once we recognized that this need was there, we all accepted the challenge. It was going to require not only an individual but a collective effort. They had to think more than ever before as a team, because these four people had a tremendously important role in our success or failure, and since we were staring failure squarely in the face, they, more than anyone, had the responsibility of turning it around."

And turn it around they did, if not to a clean-cut first, at least back to the status quo of a close race with WBZ.

There were, of course, other elements that contributed to this downward trend that had to be addressed. Balboni also met regularly with the producers and assistant producers, particularly of the six and eleven o'clock shows, to discuss such problems as a lack of consistency in the quality of production and errors, technical and human, that led to mishaps on the air.

More pervasive was, and continues to be, the formatting of newscasts resulting in clumping together too many stories of the same thrust—rapes, fires, trials, for example. This cannot always be avoided, of course. News being news, there may be a lot of violence and courtroom scenes unfolding on one single day. But extreme care must be taken, Balboni believes, to give each program as much change of pace as the news permits and always to bear in mind the vital importance of helping viewers understand the relevance of the stories.

To implement these goals, Balboni chairs a meeting every weekday morning at 9:30 at which potential stories for the six o'clock news are discussed and evaluated. Present at these sessions are the assistant news director, Emily Rooney; the senior executive producer/news programming, Charlie Kravetz; and the executive producer of the six o'clock news, Linda Polach; the sports producer; and the assignment manager, who is responsible for assembling and presenting the stories; and the assignment chief, whose job is to coordinate the field operations of the reporters, cameramen, and sound trucks and to set up all live shots.

Having "shopped" this meeting two or three times looking for a compelling, well-balanced, contentious news day to portray, I have become quite familiar with the routine.

There are usually about twenty to twenty-five stories to be considered; everyone is handed a typed list of these with the subject in capital letters, followed by a short explanatory sentence (e.g.: "GARROWAY SENTENCING, Navy could ask death penalty for black sailor who killed white officer"), and, if it is an ongoing story, the name of the reporter who is covering it.

Each story is briefly and argumentatively discussed; Balboni doesn't care much for the New Bedford fishermen's strike, Rooney says we can't just leave it hanging, Kravetz wants a reporter "baby-sitting it" in any case. To the observer (me), it seems as if they never reach a conclusion before they go on to the next item on the list.

When they have covered each story, they go through it quickly once more, and it seems they have known what they were doing the whole time.

"Let's see now, in Kater-Arruda [a particularly gruesome murder-rape case being tried for the second time] the jury has been deliberating for seven days. Jack [Harper] is covering that and we might get a verdict today. . . . Let's put Kirby [Perkins] on the *Rambo* protest at Harvard [Sylvester Stallone is being honored as "man of the year" by the Hasty Pudding Club at Harvard, and outraged embittered Vietnam veterans are planning a protest]. . . . Mary Ann [Kane] will go and see what's happening at Eastern Airlines [rumor has it they are about to declare bankruptcy]. . . . David Ropeik is following the Woburn toxic waste suit [a potential Love Canal situation]. . . . Shirley McNerney can do the new corporate day-care center in Lawrence. . . . Now what do we have for Martha [Bradlee]?"

There does not seem to be a tailor-made story for Martha's particular talents, so it seems best to have her "do" the Philippines, which she has done several times before, but there are probably going to be some new developments she can work on.

That assignment is left hanging since Martha does not come in until three in the afternoon so that she can appear on both the six and the eleven o'clock news. Someone briefly mentions the weather; in the early morning there was freezing rain, but although it is still drizzling, the temperature has warmed up, so that is considered a nonstory. Everyone agrees it looks like a very good news day.

When the meeting breaks up, I ask Phil Balboni if I may go with Kirby Perkins to watch him cover the *Rambo* protest story. Balboni says sure. Kirby is gracious, agreeing to keep me posted on his preparations during the day, as he does not plan to leave the station until late afternoon to cover the five-thirty demonstration.

Accordingly I settled down at the six o'clock pod next to executive producer Linda Polach on my right, plain producers Jim Smith and Mimi Wishner on my left. That word *executive* makes a big difference. For one thing it marks the possessor of that title as management and thus exempt from joining AFTRA or the technical union, IBEW.

Since all the top brass on this particular day happen to be at an all-day meeting, there is a feeling in the pod somewhat akin to the when-the-cat's-away atmosphere of the *Eye-opener*. After remarking with some glee on her feeling of freedom, Linda Polach gets down to business. "We have a lot of stories today—too many," she says as she prudently tries to determine which one or two might be expendable in the likelihood of something breaking as the day progresses.

To keep track of such developments she is constantly being handed a fat package of printouts—wire-service copy from the Associated Press and United Press International. With a trained eye she glances over them, and with incredible speed she throws the majority that don't interest her into a large wastecan at her side. While performing this chore with almost rhythmic regularity, she is at the same time talking to her colleagues (and graciously keeping me filled in) while also answering the phone.

Many of the calls she takes are simply people questioning some detail from an earlier broadcast or asking for general information on some topic in the news. Why interns, of which there are many, don't take care of these interruptions to an often harassed staff, I have not been able to fathom.

Around about 11:45 Polach says she should be able to make at least a pre-preliminary format of how the evening newscast will go, but today she is stumped. No lead seems to spring to the fore, a circumstance which begins to make everyone at the pod feel uneasy even though it is still early.

Meanwhile I go off to talk to Kirby Perkins about how he plans to cover the Sylvester Stallone story.

We sit down in the office of his wife, Emily Rooney, while Kirby, one of the station's most versatile and sophisticated reporters, tells me wryly that this assignment does not in his view constitute profound reporting.

Still, it is of some interest to him because he himself was a Vietnam War protester on the University of California, Berkeley, campus during the late sixties and thus relates to the antiwar veterans who are planning to demonstrate this evening.

He is preparing his coverage in two ways; one by setting up some pretaped interviews with protesting veterans, and two by putting together a fifteen-second edited spot of some of Stallone's "shlock" movies in which Rambo, speaking only in grunts, is pictured as a hero, guns wildly blazing, coming into Vietnam to rescue Americans still being tortured by the "gooks."

As one veteran has already told Kirby, "This creep was

Reporter Kirby Perkins with editor Jim Reidy

making porn movies while I was in Vietnam watching my buddies die," a line he is using in his voice-over.

He then plans to interview on the site a representative of the Hasty Pudding Club to ask if this unseemly award is for real or tongue-in-cheek. And finally, he will go "genuinely live" (as opposed to "fabricated live," which means the reporter stands at the spot where whatever he is reporting on happened earlier) at 6:15 to talk as it is actually happening to such protesters as he can manage to collar. Three minutes, ten seconds have been allotted for his story.

I arrange to meet him in front of the Hasty Pudding Club around five-thirty and go back to the six o'clock pod to see what's happening.

Still no viable lead has emerged, although many ideas are floating around. And the lead, of course, is of paramount importance—the greatest possible hedge against dial-flipping.

Polach tends to favor the heart-rending story taking place in the suburban town of Woburn, where eight families who have between them lost five children to leukemia are suing two international companies for polluting the community wells with toxic solvents. Although the case is only beginning on this day and would be no more than a table-setter, Polach has earmarked it for the lead because she predicts it might well be of national importance. But then David Ropeik, who is covering it, phones to say that since the jury selection is just beginning, no real action is expected for several weeks, which is not the stuff of which leads are made.

Attention then shifts to the horrendously damaging and dangerous floods and mudslides in the Napa Valley area of Northern California. Here one might ask the obvious question: does the lead story on a local news program have to be local? The answer, as far as this or any other top-quality station is concerned, is an emphatic no.

As Phil Balboni has stated publicly, "Local television is entering a golden age. I think the audience is more receptive to local news doing a comprehensive job of trying to bring the news of the entire world to them."

Natalie Jacobson reflects the same thought: "What happens throughout the world affects us all. And if that means entering into national and international news and trying to relate that to what is happening here at home, then we must do it."

This is true especially if a national or international story is of overriding importance to the viewers. In this regard the California story hardly qualifies, but Polach keeps pointing out, with mounting frustration, that none of the other stories under consideration, good as they may be in themselves, are truly lead stories; some may not even make the prestigious A segment of the evening newscast.

So, lacking any better candidate, she instructs Jim Smith to call San Francisco station KRON to ask if their NewsStar truck is available to provide WCVB with pictures of the mudslide. This expeditiously accomplished, Smith calls Conus to arrange for satellite time for this story but can only get it toward the end of the A segment, which he accepts but which of course knocks that idea out as a lead.

Mary Ann Kane telephones in to say that the situation at Eastern Airlines is critical; it appears they will be filing for bankruptcy in the next few days. I suspect she is angling for the lead on this, but Polach says that when they actually *do* file, it may possibly be the lead, but not now.

This then brings her with the utmost reluctance to the Kater-Arruda murder case, a story which she abhors, which Balboni hates, but which is the kind of story that all local stations have to deal with far more than they want to.

William Kater was convicted in the 1970s for the brutal murder and rape of a young schoolgirl, Mary Jane Arruda. After he had begun serving his prison sentence, his lawyer discovered that some of the information which convicted him was obtained from eyewitnesses by hypnosis. Accordingly Kater (who had pleaded guilty to an earlier rape attempt which the intended victim miraculously escaped) was granted a new trial in a new venue (Cambridge). The jurors, who do not know he was previously convicted or previously pleaded guilty to the earlier attempt, have been deliberating for seven days and are said by Jack Harper, who is covering the case, to be at an impasse. A hung jury thus looms, which could mean that this dangerous man might well go free.

Polach now has Harper beeped. He calls back to report that the judge has sent the jury back to try once more, telling them that there will never be twelve men and women tried and true who will be better qualified to reach a verdict in this case.

Given this slim thread of new material, Polach finally pencils in Kater (Remote/Jack/Cass/sot, 2:50) for the lead and goes on to make the rest of her preliminary format to follow: Garraway Trial, Cass/vo, :30; Rambo Protest Remote/Kirby Cass/sot/ Remote/guest, 3:10; Nicaragua [Reagan has asked Congress for 100 million to aid the Contras] :50; Eastern Demise, Remote/Mary Ann Cass/sot/ Remote/Wrap, 2:60; California Floods (Conus) Live NewsStar Q and A Cass/vo B roll; Tease; BREAK.

Without enthusiasm the executive producer announces that she guesses she can live with this, and I go off to see what's coming up in the Sports Department for their SportsCenter 5 segment.

I catch Mike Lynch, newly promoted from weekend to weekday sports anchor, in a slow sports news day—a rarity in Boston—so he has a few minutes to talk about the upcoming newscast. Does he, for instance have *his* lead set? Yes, as a matter of fact, he does.

Since the Celtics are playing basketball in Sacramento and the Bruins hockey in Chicago, the lead is to be the Beanpot Hockey tournament, always a very hot local item contested each year by Harvard, Boston University, Northeastern University, and Boston College. Following a report on the game, which was won the night before by Boston University, by the sports department number-two man, Jack Edwards, the game's most valuable player, the BU goalie, will be interviewed live at the station.

"So that's what we'll lead with," says Mike Lynch, a round-faced, cheerful, agreeably laid-back Harvard man who has been a sports freak all his young life. "Unless something breaks between now and six o'clock; then we'll have to reshuffle."

I ask what is likely to break on this quiet sort of day.

"You never know," he says. "At six-fifteen I've had trades announced, coaches fired, players moving from one city to another, teams being sold. It does happen, especially in this town. But if it doesn't tonight, then we go on from the Beanpot to high school basketball, covering a game between Brookline High and Cambridge Rindge. This is the time of year we can do this sort of thing. It's always deserving, but most of the time we can't fit it in."

Deserving but not very exciting, I think. Reading my thoughts, he adds that they are going to put a cameraman on the bus with Cambridge kids as they drive over to Brookline and then have a video tape of the dressing room and the pregame speeches by both coaches. "The whole taping will take two or three hours but will run two minutes."

"Out of a total of how many for the sports segment?"

"Probably seven minutes tonight. But then in a couple of weeks we'll need more time because it will be as busy as it can get. Spring training will be going on in baseball, there will be boys' and girls' high school basketball and high school hockey, college basketball playoffs, and college hockey championships to report on. The Bruins and the Celtics will both be playing, the baseball season will be just around the corner, and the Boston Marathon will be following right behind that. And we'll cover it all somehow."

"How many coverers do you have?"

"Just three of us. Myself, Jack Edwards, and weekend man Mike Dowling."

"And except on rare nights like tonight, are you always pressed for time?"

"Always. Every night we try to put a size-eleven foot into a size-eight shoe. We try to format it. They give us seven minutes and we say okay, thirty seconds for this, forty-five for that, but invariably we start to run over, and Mike Fernandez our producer yells in our earpiece from the control room: Speed it up. Drop page twenty-two, drop the Candlepin Bowling story. Wrap it up. Wrap it."

I suggest that the almost breathless pace at which they report sports often seems to give the whole show a shot in the arm.

He says he hopes so but adds, "In this town the sports fans are very sharp. They don't want to be talked *at*, they want to be talked *with*. You've got to somehow come across like maybe you're talking with them in a tavern."

"Even so, you can be talking fast."

"Yeah, right. That's how we've got to do it."

Before leaving this engaging man, I extracted from him the usual biographical information. At Harvard he played football and baseball but managed to avoid any journalistic experience either on the *Crimson* or the university radio station. After graduation his first sports job was as a spotter for the Harvard football games on radio.

After the season he earned his keep as a bartender, to his mother's dismay ("For this we sent you to Harvard?"), and came back the next football season as the "color" man. After that he was hired by a local radio station that was strong on sports, covering both the Bruins and the Red Sox. In March 1982 he joined WCVB as a freelancer to fill in on weekends. Eighteen months later he signed a three-year contract as "the Monday-to-Friday guy."

As I head back to the Newsroom I run into Linda Polach, who has been out taking a look at the weather, which is unseeable from the windowless Newsroom and is abominable—a heavy downpour. Question: will this rain freeze by six o'clock? If so, we may have a new lead.

Dick Albert, the six o'clock weatherman, is not yet back from another assignment, but one of his lieutenants is on duty and says he is almost sure the rain will not be freezing by six o'clock. He is, however, quite certain that it will be freezing later in the evening.

I look at Linda Polach; she shakes her head. "Marginal"

she says. "But still a possibility if it is actually sleeting by six."

I remark that this lead is changing as often as it does in a basketball game, and she says she doesn't ever remember a day when she had so much trouble with it.

By the time we get back to the Newsroom it changes again. As Polach picks up a new pile of wire-service copy, her eyes hit at once on the report of an explosion that has just taken place at the U.S. Embassy in Lisbon.

Everyone galvanizes. This surely *is* lead material, although the next dispatch indicates there were only minor injuries and no one was killed. It is a grisly but indisputable fact in all news, TV and print, that such a story would have been bigger and more compelling if there had been fatalities.

Nonetheless the Lisbon story is quickly written in the top spot, and by this time Martha Bradlee has arrived and is at once assigned to cover it. This makes the Lisbon incident even more "fortunate" because the Philippines story that Martha had been penciled in to deal with had not materialized into much that day, and an A segment without the chief correspondent being represented could be construed as an admission that there was no story important enough for her.

Natalie and Chet check in, and with their arrival the pace quickens. After looking over the format of the show (mercifully just finished before their arrival), Chet writes the tease of what will be seen on *NewsCenter 5 at Six*, which will be aired at 3:15. He will also do another one for 4:30. Natalie does one for 5:30.

They both appear to be quite busy at their typewriters; besides the teases, they produce all the news updates. Although they don't have enough time to write their own initial copy, they do have final editorial control over what they are going to say, and therefore will change any phraseology they don't like or argue any implication they don't agree with (a frequent occurrence, as Natalie has pointed out).

Mike Lynch with Wayne Smith in ENG Room

Jim Barker at the audio panel

Chuck Kraemer, the witty and literate critic-at-large, pokes his head in to see if his review of the new Bob Fosse musical, *Big Deal*, in Boston for its pre-Broadway tryout, is still on for tonight. Polach says yes, two minutes.

Shirley McNerney comes back from her corporate day-care center and is told she will have 1:30 on the B segment. "Even if it is worth two-fifteen?" she asks. "Even if," Polach says cheerfully. I ask Shirley, as she rummages for a stop-watch in the desk where I am sitting, if she really expected 2:15. "No, of course not." She smiles. "I was just angling for an extra ten seconds."

Charlie Kravetz comes down from the all-day meeting to see how the format is going and groans at having *Rambo* so early in the newscast. No change, however, is made.

Mary Ann Kane comes back from Eastern Airlines and seems content with her scheduled spot on the A segment.

Paula Lyons, the consumer expert, has just come back from Japan, where she filmed a four-part series. She hurries into the Newsroom, lights go on, the six o'clock pod is hastily cleared, and she tapes a twenty-second bite to introduce that evening's *Made in Japan* installment. She seems disgruntled, but everyone by then is too busy for me to ask why.

So I take my leave to go to Cambridge to meet Kirby Perkins at the Hasty Pudding Club. The narrow street on which the venerable old club stands is thick with policemen, both Cambridge city and Harvard University campus cops. The sidewalk opposite the Pudding building is roped off, and all the parking meters on the left-hand side of the one-way street are covered with No Parking signs. Yet, in typical Cambridge style, every place is taken, three of the vehicles being the trucks from the three TV stations, Channels 4, 5, and 7. With their transmitting antennas raised high, they give a strong sense of drama to a scene where so far very little is happening except an increasingly heavy downpour, which to my sensitive eyes and feet seems slightly icy.

I am glad to get out of the horrendous weather into the safety of the Channel 5 sound truck—gladder, I imagine, than the crew are to have me, for at that moment they are transmitting Kirby's first bite back to the station, and although this is of course an everyday occurrence, all of them—the cameraman, the engineer, and Kirby—seem preoccupied, even a bit tense.

But I have learned that very little that is being prepared to go on the air is ever treated as just an everyday occurrence. Tempers do fly, hair is torn, curses are shouted as glitches happen that do not seem visible to the naked eye—at least not to mine.

They are just sending back the mélange of scenes from *Rambo* with Kirby's voice-over commenting on Stallone's grunts that while "Rambo doesn't say much, his movies are nonetheless an extraordinary success. A lot of people like what they see, but on the other hand many disaffected Vietnam veterans hate it." He then quotes the "this creep was making porn movies" line, but prudently changes the characterization of "this creep" simply to "Stallone."

The next part transmitted is his interviews with two Vietnam veterans, taped before he went to the Hasty Pudding Club. These bites will be standing by at the ready until he decides exactly how he wants to coordinate them with the about-to-take-place live protest—a choice that is up to him.

While he darts off into the clubhouse to arrange for his next interview with a Hasty Pudding officer, I take advantage of the comparative lull in the proceedings and the warmth of the truck to clarify with the engineer just how this material is being sent back to the station about eighteen miles to the south in Needham.

I have already learned some of the fundamentals from Dave Folsom, Channel 5's chief engineer. I know, for instance, that there are a number of ways of sending a signal to and from the station. There is first the old-fashioned telephone longline method still occasionally used by ABC to send its signal to Boston. More and more, ABC has depended on microwave to get its signal from New York through various hops up to Boston.

As Folsom has stated, "Basically microwave means that all of this magic of TV gets sent from one point to the other over the air, as opposed to cable, in a method known as radio frequency transmission. There are a number of frequencies throughout the spectrum, and the microwave region got its name because the waves are very small."

Microwaves do not follow the curvature of the earth but pass in a straight line—a straight line of sight, that is, meaning that the source and the destination must be within unobstructed sight of each other (if one could see that far). One of Dave Folsom's jobs is to calculate that path.

Signals from Boston to the station (and vica versa) go from the source to the top of the Prudential Building (at the edge of Copley Square) and from there to a ninety-foot tower that sticks up in back of the Needham station high enough to provide the line of sight from the Prudential. There are three microwave antennas on this tower: one for receiving the network signal and the other two for receiving WCVB's news microwave signal.

But there is yet another and ever more prevalent method, which transmits a live signal via satellite. In TV parlance this is referred to as an uplink between the earth and the sky. The satellite receives the signal, then rebroadcasts it down to earth, where stations pick it up on huge dishes they have in their back lots. These huge dishes, acting as both receiver and transmitter, also send the signal up to the satellite.

Until comparatively recently the satellite dishes installed at the TV station were stationary; they could not be transported to other locations to shoot live remotes. In 1985, however, Channel 5 became only the second station in the country to acquire a portable satellite transmitting and receiving station. NewsStar 5, its fabulous truck complete with a very high-performance dish and all the necessary satellite technology, also includes an editing suite. (It sounds as if it should be as big as a Greyhound bus, but it is in fact only about the size of an ordinary delivery truck.)

NewsStar makes it possible to transmit from anywhere in the continental United States that the truck can drive to. And what makes satellite technology so remarkable is that no matter where one transmits from in the United States, the signal is still the same because the satellite is so far away that it stays in relatively the same position. All of this makes for enormous mobility in live remotes. As an example, Dave Folsom points out, "If a plane crashed out in the middle of nowhere and there was some little dirt road so we could drive NewsStar up to it, we could come from there live."

And yet it is obviously not expedient to book expensive satellite time to transmit a signal that can just as well go by microwave. So although NewsStar 5 is about as state-of-the-art as you can get, it does not have the plain old state-of-*yesterday's*-art microwave transmitter to cover local stories, as does the truck, Zebra, in which I am sitting.

To send Kirby's first taped bites back to the station, Zebra has raised its pole antenna to its full fifty feet, which gives it line of sight to the Prudential, from where the signal is sent in milliseconds, again by line of sight to the station.

The same procedure will be repeated when Kirby covers the protesting demonstrators live, with one exception. For that bite his mike will be attached by cable to the Zebra and will go from there directly with no tapes involved.

This clarified, I wait for Kirby to come back, which he does on the run, demanding that the cameraman follow him into the clubhouse to tape his interview with the Hasty Pudding Theatricals president.

I tag along for this leg of the journey. After some delay, while another station finishes its interview, Kirby holds the

Channel 5 microphone toward the young president and delicately suggests that this award has sometimes been given with "shall we say satirical intent. Is that the case this year?"

With extreme earnestness Joshua Berger denies the very idea of such a cynical thought and insists that this is a truly serious award. In fact, he says, "We had a seminar with Mr. Stallone today, and he just charmed the pants off all of us at the Hasty Pudding. A wonderfully witty, humorous man."

By the time we get back to the street the protesters have started to assemble on the sidewalk opposite the club, sloshing their way through the increasing cold, sleety downpour. The atmosphere is not confrontational and under the circumstances seems relatively good-natured, especially as "Mr." Stallone is not yet on hand to hear the jibes being chanted against him. ("Rambo is not our Man of the Year.")

Kirby hurries over to Zebra, where the engineer is uncoiling the cable, and then I lose him as he mingles in the crowd of perhaps seventy-five hardy, protesting souls.

I stand for about ten minutes or so watching the scene, feeling miserably wet and cold, until, glancing at my watch, I realize that if I go now I shall be able to see it all in far greater comfort on television in my own living room. And so, slipping and sliding toward my illegally parked car, I cut and run.

I get home just as the Boston skyline opening of *NewsCenter 5 at Six* flashes on the screen, and I swear everyone in my family to silence as I watch unfold what by now feels to me like the fruits of my own hard day's labor. Silently I make a bet with myself about the lead. And I win.

Chet teases: "An ice storm causes power outages in several communities, and that's our first report." The broadcast begins, and popular weatherman Dick Albert comes on announcing, "Many reports of heavy rain falling below freezing. . . . It is icing up very rapidly. . . . The trees are really drooping. . . . This could be a serious ice storm as the rain keeps pelting down and the ice keeps building up. . . . We will keep you posted."

So the dark horse icing story did after all win the lead sweepstakes.

Knowing that the format when I left the station called for the Lisbon Embassy bomb to lead, I now expect that story to follow. But no, damned if Kater-Arruda doesn't come next. I am perplexed as to why it topped Lisbon until I see that Jack Harper has managed an interview with Mrs. Arruda, the mother of the victim, who, faced with the possibility of a hung jury, bravely asserts that she will call for yet another trial and go through all that agony for the third time to ensure that Kater remains in prison.*

Then comes Lisbon, which seems after all not so much of a story except that Martha Bradlee does a good job of sketching the three previous attacks on that embassy in the last two years. She then talks by phone (with the map of Spain and Portugal from the Electronic Still Store displayed on the screen) with an AP reporter in Lisbon who was an eyewitness to the incident of the car blowing up after its owner, sensing trouble, had gotten out. As yet there are no clues. In the previous attempts a group called ST–25 claimed responsibility.

On to the president's request for $100 million for Nicaraguan Contras with network footage of Reagan at the White House talking to top Republicans on the screen as Natalie reads thirty seconds of copy.

And then finally Chet introduces the Rambo protest. Naturally, I have a proprietary feeling toward this story and am particularly curious as to how Kirby Perkins is going to put all his diverse elements together in the comparatively long three minutes, ten seconds allotted to him.

---

*He was found guilty by the jury the next day in time for the Midday News.

On the screen it looks deceptively simple. He comes on live, holding an umbrella as the protesters, also holding umbrellas, march back and forth behind him, chanting anti-Rambo sentiments. He sets the scene quickly, then loses the protesters to go to his *Rambo* film bite with his voice-over, wipes to his two taped interviews with disgruntled veterans, next to his sharply contrasting bite with the president of the Hasty Pudding Theatricals. Back to the live—real live—shot again of protesters marching while, with them moving up and down behind him, he interviews an articulate and outraged member of Boston's Asian-American community. He wraps with the information that the great Sylvester Stallone will be arriving in approximately one half-hour. Then: "Live from Cambridge, this is Kirby Perkins, NewsCenter Five. Back to you, Chet." Time, three minutes, eleven seconds. One second over. Talk about professional!

Thus endeth the A segment.

Not until the middle of the commercial do I realize that they have missed their satellite time for the California mudslide. As it turns out, that story is reduced to a mere mention during the slightly expanded weather section. Also, Mary Ann Kane did not make the A segment, but opens the B along with David Ropeik on Woburn's toxic waste suit and Shirley McNerny with her one minute, thirty seconds on the corporate day-care center.

In fact, the show runs along after the first break more or less as anticipated, the sports segment being as uninspiring as I thought it might be (but deserving), Paula Lyons being as briskly informative (how many local stations even have a consumer reporter, much less one they send to Japan for a report?), and Chuck Kraemer as incisive about *Big Deal*. "It isn't yet," he suggests, "and needs to be renegotiated before it gets to Broadway."

And I know, since I have been there numerous times before at this hour, how the control room must have been buzzing with what Chet calls the pressure-cooker factor. "Dissolve to graphic. . . . Roll four, take it. . . . Still Store up. . . . Track five, do it! . . . Camera 2 on Natalie and zoom. . . . Stand by for tease. . . . "

The next day I telephone Linda Polach to thank her for being so helpful to me and also to gloat that I was sure she was going to wind up with the lead she finally did.

"What *did* we lead with last night?" she says. "I forget."

Yesterday's news! Nothing could be staler. Now it's today, and today's news must be as fresh and appealing as newly baked bread.

———

7

Prime Access: *Chronicle*, 7:30 to 8:00 P.M.

CHRONICLE IS THE PRO-
gram that more than any other distinguishes Channel 5 from
every other local television station in the country. Produced
entirely in-house, it deals with a single substantive subject
every evening between 7:30 and 8:00 in what is called prime
access or local access time.

To appreciate the importance of *Chronicle* one must first
understand the significance of that prime/local access time.

In the early 1970s, when the FCC was considerably more
gritty than the rubber stamp outfit it has since become, the
commission made a bold move designed to encourage local
broadcasting. It took the 7:30–8:00 P.M. slot away entirely
from the networks and designated it as prime access time.
The clear aim was to foster locally produced initiatives in
this important period between the news and the start of
prime time.

But what happened was that instead of innovative programming, most stations throughout the country simply

slapped a non-network syndicated show into the time period, thus fulfilling the letter of the law.

WCVB, Channel 5, made an effort to respect the *spirit* of the law by devising a local format of sorts in what is called a checkerboard pattern—that is, having a different program each of the five nights, but always having the same one on the same night in the tradition of "If this is Thursday, there must be a medical program on Channel 5." There was some syndicated material in the mix—for example, *The Muppets* on Tuesday—and such was the hodgepodge that the entire show was difficult to market and did not do well in the ratings.

That was in the BBI days, and they were willing to tolerate this loss for a while, but Philip Balboni, then director of public affairs, believed some serious thought should be put into the most important time period controlled by the station apart from local news.

He began his thinking by opting for an alternative format to checkerboarding called strip programming, meaning the same program every night, a concept he felt would build consistency of viewing and easier promotion in marketing.

On the first day of December 1980, Balboni launched his trial balloon for prime access in a memo recommending a series to be produced jointly by the News and Public Affairs departments which would contain three or four principal elements:

1. Straight news, recapping in three to five minutes the top local stories of the day
2. In-depth magazine-style reports on interesting local or regional topics
3. A live remote on a major event unfolding that day, whenever appropriate
4. A special thematic segment which would be regularly featured each night of the week

Bob Bennett responded with his characteristic enthusiasm to Balboni's proposal and shortly began a process of evaluating and refining it with BBI's Board of Directors and with the sales staff. Jim Thistle, at that time head of news, and Paul La Camera, in charge of public affairs, had both been consulting with Balboni from the beginning.

In August 1981, after nine months of gestation, Bennett gave his final approval to the still unnamed program.

"It was a great article of faith on Bob's part," says Balboni, "because no program of this sort had ever before been attempted. The closest thing to it was *60 Minutes* on CBS. Our program was very expensive; it represented a new million-dollar investment on the station's part and the hiring of substantial numbers of people. There was no pilot. We never did do a pilot. It was all on paper and in conversation."

Charlie Kravetz, who had been the producer of a successful several-times-a-year prime-time show called *Calendar*, and Judy Stoia, who produced specials, were made co-equals with the respective titles of Producer and Managing Editor, with Balboni the Executive Producer. On January 25, 1982, the finally named *Chronicle* made its debut accompanied by a burst of carefully planned publicity.

But despite the fanfare, or perhaps even because of it, *Chronicle* proved a disappointment. The ratings, which started out high, probably because of the pre-opening hoopla, fell precipitously, and the feedback from both critics and audience was that the show was not living up to its potential.

Airing opposite the successful if light and fluffy *Evening Magazine* on WBZ (and on all other Westinghouse stations), *Chronicle* made what may have appeared a rather self-conscious attempt to be "substantive" at all costs, particularly in the A segment, which was looked upon as serious, thoughtful news and/or public affairs oriented.

The second segment, possibly with an eye on *Evening*

Magazine's lighter approach, was "more feature-oriented" says Kravetz, and looking back on it he thinks the juxtaposition of these two segments was jarring.

A further problem was that they did not have enough material, owing to limitations in staff and know-how in the magazine format, to fill the third segment. So they used a syndicated travelogue called *News Travel Network*, which didn't fit with either of the first two segments. More and more the critics savaged them (and the ratings reflected this) for promising so much and producing so ineffectively.

"*Chronicle* tried to please everybody," says Kravetz, "and it didn't even please *us*, although at the time we didn't know why. Now I realize that it didn't have a sense of purpose, except maybe to cover all bases. In trying to be all things to all people, you wind up aiming for the lowest common denominator. And that really wasn't in keeping with who we were."

All this analysis is, of course, hindsight. At the time they were never so clear about what the underlying problems really were. And in point of fact *who* they were changed quite radically when *Chronicle* was only a few months old. In May of 1982 WCVB was acquired by Metromedia, whose past history did not encourage those in charge of *Chronicle* to think that their new owners would long be as permissive as the avuncular BBI had been, about a low-rating show and a critical failure to boot, running in prime access time.

Concurrent with the change of management, although not necessarily because of it, Jim Thistle left the station (and the world of TV altogether), and Phil Balboni was tapped to be his successor as head of news. In the same musical-chairs fashion, Paul La Camera was promoted to head of programming, and S. James Coppersmith, who had wide experience as a general manager in four important markets (including Boston, where he had run Channel 7), was brought in to assume those duties at WCVB, Bob Bennett, in his round of musical chairs, having stepped up to president of Metromedia Television.

Jim Coppersmith says although *Chronicle* may not have been in any imminent danger, he did have to fight to keep it afloat, but knowing how easy it would be to put a "rating grabber" into the spot, he admits he did find himself vacillating from time to time. This unworthy thought surfaced one day at a staff meeting when he heard himself say, "We could just put a game show in there and make a fortune." Paul La Camera shot him a hard look and then said quietly, "Jim, you didn't come back to Boston to run a game show at seven-thirty at night."

"That simple sentence and the way he looked at me hit me like a sledgehammer," says Coppersmith. "After that I never wavered in my conviction that *Chronicle* could and should be the best thing ever seen on local television."

Through most of the summer of '82, Paul La Camera, Charlie Kravetz, and Judy Stoia puzzled and agonized over why their (and Balboni's) brainchild had turned into such an ugly duckling.

"We did a lot of brooding," says Judy Stoia. "I remember how Charlie and I sat on my back porch saying over and over, 'What are we doing wrong?' We knew we were missing but we didn't know why. And you know it's very hard to fix things in public. It's also hard to grow up in public."

And then, as so often happens during the growing-up process, maturity came quite by accident. During that summer the subject of drinking and driving began to occupy more and more attention, and responding to this new public consciousness, La Camera and his colleagues decided to deviate from the *Chronicle* formula and devote an entire program to this compelling subject. "It felt good," says La Camera. So good in fact that they decided to do another single-theme show—on police brutality—and then still another, on a cruel racial incident in the Hyde Park section of Boston.

Each of these half-hours felt right—"fulfilling" (La Camera's word)—and offered a promise of that sense of purpose they had all been seeking. And at the same time came a lot of strong positive feedback from previously stern critics. Stoia remembers a friend of hers calling from the Kennedy School of Government and saying in an it's-about-time voice, "Well, finally I think you've got it right."

So the decision was made to go to a one-subject-a-night format with programs ranging from the most late-breaking news to more feature-oriented material. Without the forced juxtaposition of topics, they hoped that viewers would leave the program with enough substance to be intellectually satisfied.

Concurrent with this major change, La Camera, Kravetz, and Stoia also decided to stop preparing their programs so far in advance in order to be more responsive to topical stories. So instead of looking at their schedule on a Monday morning and seeing a program go into the works that would not be aired for two or three weeks, they would, when the situation warranted it, start a program on Monday that would air on Friday or Wednesday or even, in the case of a major, fast-breaking story, that very same Monday night.

In the beginning, right after the transition, they in fact tended to overemphasize hard news, and it wasn't until they felt a little more secure with their new product that they branched out into cultural and lifestyle pieces as well.

One further advantage of the one-topic-a-night format was that it forced those in charge to choose subjects of substance, since by definition the subject had to be one that would merit and *require* a half-hour's time.

It would be gratifying to report that the change in style and content of the program was at once reflected in a significant upward swing in the ratings. However, it was not.

Mary Richardson   Peter Mehegan

As with network magazine shows, it took several years for
Chronicle to find its local level, which by 1986 it finally had.
With an average rating of 9, it still does not win its time
period but remains second to *Evening Magazine* (with a 12
rating) and beats Channel 7's syndicated *Entertainment Tonight* (7 rating).

Advertisers have been loyal and supportive even during
the program's darkest days; True Value Hardware has been
a sponsor since the beginning, and others are glad to latch
on to an offering they look on as prestigious with the promise
of attracting the kind of viewers they hope to reach. So
Chronicle's commercial as well as its cultural value has been
more than satisfying. Jim Coppersmith refers to it as "a little
business we'd all like to have a piece of," and the gossip in
this station where dollars and cents are rarely articulated is
that the show makes a million dollars a year.

• • •

Today *Chronicle* has twelve field producers, most of whom work on a regular schedule of one segment each for six days. There are two scripted segments; the third is usually a commentary. Roughly this works out to two days to do what they call setting up, meaning planning, then making the arrangements for materials to be taped; one day to shoot the segment; one day to screen and transcribe tapes; one day to write; and one day, the sixth, to edit. Since editing more often than not comes on the day of airing, it is usually the most tense time for the field producers and their ever-calming video editors.

Included in these twelve field producers are the two regular anchors: the gifted, quick-witted Peter Mehegan, as Irish as his name, and the composed, intelligent Mary Richardson. These two are the versatile old pros of the staff; as well as anchoring the program, they are responsible for producing their own segments, which are many and varied. Mary Richardson has in the space of six months been to both China and Ireland to bring back stories, and Peter Mehegan to Africa. Much of the success of *Chronicle* depends on their talent and craftsmanship.

Their backup is a young black woman named Andria Hall,* who is widely looked upon as a comer. In fact, Paul La Camera calls her a "star in the making," a word she says bothers her; she feels it connotes a person set apart—aloof.

Andria qualifies both as a role model and as an exemplar of *Chronicle*, the insider through whose eyes we might now have a look at the program.

At age twenty-nine, southern-born but raised in Brooklyn, Andria's career has hardly been stereotypical, first because she fell into television by accident, and second because all

*"Be sure you spell my name right," Andria Hall admonished me. "My mother spelled it wrong because she really thought *Andria* was spelled with an *i*, but I've always been very particular about sticking to her spelling, right or wrong."

Chronicle's Andria Hall

of her jobs, culminating in this, her fourth position in as many cities, have come very easily to her.

"Certainly mine has not been the story of struggle and suffering," she says ruefully. "Yes, I *do* think being black has been an advantage, but even if you may get hired because you're black, you don't *stay* hired because you're black. If I didn't know what I was doing, I wouldn't be here in Boston in the sixth market in the country."

Nor would she be holding down the sort of position she has on *Chronicle*, where she actually wears three hats, primarily as an on-air reporter, then as a field producer, and finally as a frequent anchorperson.

In a characteristic day not long ago, Andria spent the morning as a reporter for a show being shot at Boston's Children's Hospital by Assistant Program Producer Bob Geballe. He had her come to the hospital to do an interview with a Dr. Jones, who was about to perform complicated knee surgery on a ten-year-old boy, Michael. Although Geballe could, as field producer, interview the doctor himself, his voice could not be heard on the air since Geballe is not "talent."† Therefore, he would have had to tip off the doctor to answer his question as if he were making a statement. But since Andria was to be doing the "track work" or voice-over part of the segment, Geballe felt it was important for the viewer to see her on the site of Children's Hospital. So she both interviewed Dr. Jones and did a "stand-up" in the lobby of the hospital.

That was her morning. In the afternoon she went, as it happened, to yet another hospital, again as talent, this time for another producer, to shoot the dieting segment of a show on fitness and dieting. The following day, as field producer herself, she shot the fitness part of the program, so her voice was heard on both segments, although she acted in a different capacity in each.

She begins her fitness segment with an opening sequence of a young Oriental man in the magnificent Arnold Arboretum practicing the seven-hundred-year-old Chinese form of graceful exercise known as T'ai Chi. She then moves to present-day aerobics—a pop culture, she says in her stand-up—and on to a new craze called the Swimmex, in which a generator in a small pool produces a fast-flowing stream against which the swimmer seems to be swimming miles while staying in the same place. She winds up with a timely warning about overdoing exercises and about the importance of having a safe aerobic instructor trained in body mechanics.

Two days later having first screened this piece, a tedious

---

†The distinction is important for more than just strategic reasons. On-air persons are paid almost twice as much as field producers whose average salary is said to be "in the mid-thirties."

job involving putting all the tapes—two to three hours' worth—on the monitor and recording the concurrent sounds and dialogue she wishes to use, and having then written the script and had it approved by either Producer Mark Mills or Managing Editor Susan Sloane, Andria is ready to spend the day editing. And a long day it is too; a rule of thumb has it that it takes one hour to edit one minute of air time.

The intricacies of the art of editing are bewildering to the spectator. Almost as if playing an instrument, the editor's hands fly over the banks of keys on awesome-looking panels. (Editors, by the way, are paid more than field producers but less than on-air talent.) And as I watch this millisecond timing, which can literally take the words out of a person's mouth, it strikes me that such facility could be dangerous. Consider how easily a spoken sentence—"He was afraid of not being liked"—can with a few deft twists of the editor's wrist become, "He was not liked." But fortunately this does not happen, whether because of legal constraints or pure professionalism, I'm not sure. What does happen is magic.

Andria is called away for a moment by Mark Mills, and I wander into the next editing suite to watch Bob Geballe and Kathy McKenna deal with a segment on the T—Boston's subway system. Two things are quickly pointed out to me: the audio dominates the edit, and there are only two audio tracks. And what Geballe and McKenna then have is Peter Mehegan's voice-over on one track and music on the other. The music is especially important at this stage of editing because it is used to help decide where to put what picture and for how long.

But when they have the video shots arranged to their satisfaction, they still need one more audio, which is the all-important *natural sounds*—endemic to taped television but perhaps not recognized by the viewer as such, so easily do these sounds merge into the background. To accommodate natural sounds on their two tracks, which at that point are full of Peter Mehegan's voice and music, they take the music, which for the moment has served its purpose, *off* the second track and put the natural sounds onto it. They then "mix down" these two audios—Peter's voice and natural sounds—onto one track and then put the music back on the other.

Andria comes back looking rather frazzled; Mills has just told her she will have to anchor that night because Mary Richardson, who is shooting in Philadelphia, cannot get back in time. Fortunately Mills had warned her that this might happen so she says at least she didn't come to work wearing a white blouse, thought to be glaring on the screen, or some other unsuitable top.‡ However, her hair, which she is wearing pulled rather severely straight back, will have to be a little softer, and it will take her at least ten minutes to get her makeup "camera-ready."

All she knows so far about the evening's *Chronicle* is that it "profiles" the three families who are the focal points of Anthony Lucas's National Book Award–winning book *Common Ground*. She will not have a chance to do more than look over the material very quickly since she is due on the set at 7:30 and knows they will not have finished typing up the teleprompter script much before 7:00. Unless it is absolutely unavoidable, however, she at least won't have to go on the air cold, as she has had to do on one or two hair-raising occasions.

In the course of the next few weeks, while I was following her varied activities, Andria anchored often, either while Mary Richardson was shooting in Ireland or Peter Mehegan was on vacation. As anchor she did such shows as *Kids on the Fast Track*, which explored the question of whether we rob our children of their childhood by pushing them toward

‡Natalie Jacobson's and Mary Richardson's clothes are lent to them—five costumes weekly—by shops, which are credited, rather unsuitably it seems to me, each evening. But Andria does not have her clothes sponsored, although she does receive a clothing allowance.

overachievement; *Nightline*, a behind-the-scenes look at the popular Ted Koppel show; the Republican State Convention in Worcester interviewing the gubernatorial candidates (both sure to lose in this predominantly Democratic state); a look at the understaffed, underfinanced, but still doughty Fernald School for the mentally retarded; and a show on marriage, which started rather lightly as an audience catcher but then went into a more serious segment about the problems of stepchildren. She did voice-overs for a program devoted to June graduates; a Segment Three commentary on the mystique of the Boston Garden, the city's venerable sports arena and the home of the championship Celtics; a segment on Soviet Jews for a *World of Difference* show. (*World of Difference* is Channel 5's long-running public service program against discrimination. Run in conjunction with the Anti-Defamation League and financed in part by the Shawmut Bank, it has presented literally hundreds of short spots dramatizing the evils and folly of prejudice.)

Also on the subject of discrimination, she both narrated and appeared in a program about America's newest immigrants and newest dreamers of the American dream, the Cambodians. Reporting from the coastal city of Revere, Andria's voice-over decried "no liberty or justice" for the community of one thousand much-maligned Cambodians who settled there. This particular show utilized all four of *Chronicle*'s featured "talent." Mary Richardson and Peter Mehegan anchored. Mike Barnicle, a *Boston Globe* columnist who appears on *Chronicle* several times a week, is a gifted but controversial figure, "easy to dislike, but hard not to admire," says one critic. He added a bitter Segment Three on another case of blatant discrimination against an aspiring Cambodian.

Again as reporter and talent, Andria went to picture-postcard-pretty Rockport on Cape Ann, north of Boston, to work on a program for *Chronicle*'s series *Main Streets and Back Roads*. But in this instance field producer Chris Sterling was hit with a severe stomach virus during the first day of shoot-ing, and Andria had to take over his duties as well as her own, more or less making it up as she went along, she ob-serves, but still coping. Coping is, in fact, an operational word for Andria; she has to do a lot of it in her job.

As reporter and talent but once again slipping over into field producer, she worked on a story on minorities in cor-porate Boston, posing the question of whether they have fared as well as they could have in management positions. The answer appears to be no, but the piece focuses largely on a controversy between a group of Boston's most promi-nent businessmen, always referred to as the Vault, who claim that with approximately four hundred minorities in manage-ment positions, the answer should be yes, and the Civil Rights Coalition, which insists that the management posi-tions held by minorities are not at a high enough level.

Andria became rather more involved in this case than she usually does in someone else's shoot, and, working on her own with the encouragement of field producer Rita Thomp-son, she found one stunning success story: a young man who she thinks may well be the highest-placed black in the coun-try, working for the Shawmut Bank and overseeing a budget of $8 billion.

Probably the program she produced that gave her the most trouble and the most ultimate satisfaction was *Women in Prison*, a look inside Massachusetts Correction Institution (MCI) Framingham, the state's only penitentiary for women.

When Andria was first given the assignment, it was with the understanding that she would have the show ready to air in ten broadcast days, which because of her multiple roles is her usual schedule. This time, however, the ten days stretched to more than a month because, as Andria found out, you don't just call the public relations officer and say, "Hello, I'm from Channel 5 and we want to come in and shoot some scenes from your prison next Thursday at nine-thirty," delicately implying in your tone how lucky they are to be going on television.

With the MCI Framingham story she had to submit a written proposal stating specifically what she needed and what angles she thought would be best for the show.

Knowing that Andria had never been in this or any other prison, I wondered how she could visualize what she wanted. "You know the elements you need," she told me. "I knew I wanted to find a mother who had maybe given birth to a child in prison, because that's very common, and who was getting out soon. I also knew I wanted to find a woman who was pregnant and who had a drug or an alcohol problem that would require her child to go through some detoxification program. Most important, I was working with the AIM people, which means Aid to Incarcerated Mothers, a nonprofit organization that, among other services, brings the children to Framingham by bus each Wednesday to visit with their mothers."

"But how did you even know about such an organization?" I asked her.

"You work the phones. You make one phone call, and that leads to another and another. It's all a very logical progression."

Finally, after several conversations with the public relations woman and after a second written proposal was submitted and agreed to, the shoot was set up. Field producer Pat Bates was to do the first overview, or survey segment with Andria's voice-over, and Andria would produce and voice the second segment on mothers in prison.

Especially moving and powerful are her scenes with Linda Minot, a mother of four who gave birth to her youngest, a boy, while serving a two- to four-year sentence for larceny. As her painful story unfolds—the father of the oldest child was strangled in a racial incident in college when Linda Minot was only sixteen years old and eight months pregnant, after which she says she "just went the wrong way"—the video is on a group of about fifteen young children climbing out of a van and filing into the prison, romping, skipping, and seemingly at home. Andria's voice-over as they are being searched, before going on to visit with their mothers: "Prisoners themselves, serving sentences for crimes they didn't commit."

The body of the work—that is, the seven-minute body—touches on the depressing problems of drugs—90 percent of the inmates have had substance abuse; the terrible wrench suffered by mothers who have their babies while incarcerated and then more often than not give them up either for adoption or to a foster home; the likely disruptive effect on the children's behavior if the mother returns repeatedly to prison, and the lack of support services on the outside, which makes recidivism all too probable.

The piece ends with Minot gently pushing her oldest child in a rocking chair. The little girl is kneeling toward the high back of the chair facing her mother, who leans over, kisses her daughter, then rests her chin on the top of the rocker, looking incredibly sad and wistful.

"The mother's face tells it all," says Andria. "And to capture that moment, which isn't manipulating the audience but rather letting them experience some of the emotion that is felt by these women, I put a little flute music under and held on that poignant shot of the mother."

In many ways *Chronicle* is an exemplar of Channel 5 itself in that it strives for both quality television and commercial success without sacrificing one for the other.

Producer Mark Mills says, "A program at that access time is a valuable piece of property. It's like in Monopoly. If you were in real estate, the seven-thirty hour would be Park Place. It has to make a lot of money, and *Chronicle* does. Even though we don't win the time period, we make money because we have the very classy, well-educated kind of audience that a lot of advertisers want."

"How do you know that about your audience?" I ask.

"Well, for one thing," says Mills, "you'll see a lot of big-ticket items being advertised. A lot of cars, stockbrokers, airline travel, real estate. I mean those are geared for a higher-income audience, and advertisers will pay a lot to get on our show to reach those viewers."

There seems a sort of tail-wagging-the-dog aspect about this reasoning. It causes me to wonder if Mills and Managing Editor Susan Sloane might not be making their assumptions about the high quality of their audience based on the presumed high quality of the products the advertisers are advertising on the program. In other words, if stockbrokers and travel agents are advertising on *Chronicle*, therefore *Chronicle* must have a higher-income audience with money to invest and/or education to enjoy a trip to Europe.

To try to get to the bottom of this, I take another tack, suggesting that when I studied the sweep books for demographics, I did not see any columns devoted to either income or education. So again I ask how they know they have the kind of audience they say they have. Their answer is evasive—not, I believe because they are trying to keep some state secret from me but because they aren't really sure of the facts themselves. "You'd better ask the sales department," they tell me.

Perhaps noting my doubtful look, Mark Mills says, "I think the sum of it is intuitive. If you've got *Entertainment Tonight* on Channel 7 and *Evening Magazine* on Channel 4 and you've got *Chronicle* on our station, then you can be sure a higher level of education will gravitate to us. But the sales department can give you more exact information."

I try the sales department in the person of Andy Hoffman, in charge of national sales, and find him also using the word *intuitive* and referring me to the research department for

Bob Geballe and Mary Richardson

more precise details.** I therefore suggest that perhaps the best thing I can say on this subject is that assessing the *quality* of an audience is rather an inexact science, although one that more or less works. He agrees.

But no matter how "upscale" the audience appears to be, there is a delicate balance in programming. The thing that Mark Mills, Susan Sloane, Mary Richardson, Peter Mehegan, Bob Geballe, Senior Producer Jerry Kirschenbaum, Paul La Camera, and Judy Stoia must constantly address is how to keep up revenue while presenting a program that promulgates timely, substantive ideas.

"One thing we know," says Mills, "is that we can't come in five nights a week with what Judy describes as an 'eat

---

**See the last chapter, "Sign-off."

your vegetables' kind of show: Watch it; it's good for you. So we won't go three nights in a row with South Africa, the new tax proposals, or the latest Supreme Court decision. We've got to give our audience some fun along the way."

As a matter of fact, fun is an element I find in somewhat short supply in the *Chronicle* offices and among the staff of more than thirty persons. To be sure, the pressure of producing a half-hour magazine-type show five nights a week is intense, but so is the pressure, albeit different, of putting on a newscast. Yet the atmosphere in the Newsroom is almost boisterous compared to the gravity at *Chronicle*. Staffers in the Newsroom do look up from their typewriters, smile, make comments and wisecracks, mutter oaths or shout complaints. At *Chronicle* most people seem, and probably are, so preoccupied that one hesitates to speak for fear of breaking a critical train of thought.

It is true, according to Mark Mills, that front-line field producers have such a vivid sense of purpose and perfectionism—a tunnel vision about their own particular project of the moment—that they are not keenly concerned with the overall business aspects of the program. And in a way, says Mills, who was himself a field producer (as was Susan Sloane) before taking over on the management side, that is as it should be.

But if the staff often seems fragmented and each into their own thing, when *Chronicle* undertakes a same-day effort, many of them must perforce take up an oar in one scull to get an event which unfolds during the daytime onto the screen by that evening.

A case in point is the annual Boston Marathon, a day of air effort, but one planned in advance, as opposed to an unexpectedly breaking story.

At Mills's suggestion I go to the station in the late afternoon of Marathon Day to observe (silently) the proceedings up to and including air time.

It is 5:30 and Andria is editing her piece on her colleague Laurie George, a *Chronicle* field producer who has run in the marathon. Andria was at the scene with one of three camera crews used by *Chronicle* that day (one borrowed from the Newsroom) to shoot the start of the race at Hopkinton, from Laurie George's point of view. She will pick Laurie up later at Heartbreak Hill and again at the finish line, and while there she will ask a few questions on air of other runners.

As I go into the editing room, Andria's voice is on the audio track saying, "Laurie finds herself just as serious about running as she is about her job at *Chronicle*," and Andria live, cooperative as always, stops to tell me that what she and editor Kathy McKenna are doing is "intercutting with a B roll." Now, B rolls have been explained to me many times, but always in slightly different ways, so what I have finally concluded is that a B roll is any video shot that is *not* in the situation of the moment. Thus the shot being "inter-cut" is of Laurie George, earphones on head, earnestly sitting at her desk at *Chronicle* and screening a tape, which since the situation of the moment is Laurie George at Hopkinton, Massachusetts, getting ready to run the marathon, makes this a perfect example of a B roll.

With time creeping up (this is certainly no day to adhere to the classic one hour to edit one minute of playing time), the momentum picks up swiftly in the editing suite.

Audio: "Laurie has been training easily, but this year she has a bit of extra cargo."

Video: Laurie George wearing a T-shirt that says *Baby on Board* on the front, and *Mom-To-Be* on the back. So now we know. Laurie is five months pregnant.

Video and Audio: Andria interviewing Laurie at the scene, asking about possible effects on the baby of her running a marathon. Laurie: "Well, obviously, as one doctor told me, it could be an unknown factor, since the pool of pregnant women running in a marathon is fairly small." However, the camera now picks up a man in a green T-shirt with *Dr. Bob* written on it. Dr Bob is established as an obstetrician who is going to run with Laurie and who tells us that there is no risk to his patient or her child as long as she has continued to train every day, drinks plenty of water, and doesn't press for time.

Video: Laurie kisses her husband goodbye. Long shot of the ten-thousand-plus runners lined up. Camera picks up Laurie obviously at the back of the pack. Close-up of her feet looking very tiny; gun for the start, and an endearing shot of Laurie jumping up and down in anticipation of her race.

This sequence completed, there is a great deal of squealing noise in the editing room as the tape runs backward and forward. Andria explains that they are trying to match a close-up of Laurie's legs running to a shot of *all* of Laurie running. As this effort becomes unnerving, I leave to see what's going on elsewhere in the offices of *Chronicle*. The time is now 6:45.

Peter Mehegan is in earphones rerunning the first half of the NewsCenter 5 at Six, which of course features the marathon, and taking notes. He is joined by a smallish man wearing a black-and-white striped sports shirt whom I have never seen before and to whom Peter seems to be giving some instructions. Susan Sloane, looking glassy-eyed, talks in a worried tone with intern Georgia Pappas about the fact that they do not yet have their crossplug ready. I have no idea what a crossplug is and don't dare ask, but subsequently find that it is *Chronicle*'s term for the tease for the next night's program. Peter hurries past and grins cheerfully. "Organized confusion," he says over his shoulder, then adds, "Only more screwed up than usual." Mark Mills dashes purposefully out of his office wearing a raincoat and beret, and in answer to my questioning look explains that he can just make it home to see the program from there. Director David Lawless pokes his head in and says, "Seven-fourteen," to no one in particular. Andria is still in the editing suite, and I worry about her running so close to zero hour. I go along to the control room, where Lawless is calling into his mike, "Studio control to remote three." Mike Barnicle comes on the screen from the Eliot Lounge, long a favorite with marathoners for postrace celebration. "Studio control to remote two." Remote 2 is the finish line at the John Hancock, sponsors of the race, where Mary Richardson is live. She looks unruffled as always and is given a roll cue. "Lock your shot," says Lawless. "One minute, five seconds to go." Susan Sloane takes her place at the control desk, and Andria joins me, smiling and nodding serenely to indicate all is well. The countdown: "Five, four, three, two, one—"

From the studio Peter's image comes on the one of six television screens which has the red light indicating the on-air picture. "Good evening. The ninetieth BAA Marathon takes a run for the money and comes up a winner." He teases what is ahead on the program, followed by the *Chronicle* logo and the billboard with framed pictures of Mary, Peter, Andria, and Mike Barnicle flying onto the screen. Peter throws to Mary with "At this moment the winners are still basking in the day's glory at the John Hancock Hall, where Mary Richardson is live at the award ceremony."

Mary is live, but shouldn't be because, as she says to open her bit, "The award ceremony is breaking up, and there are just a few stray picture takers around." Better, it would seem, to have put her on tape a few moments earlier to cover the actual award ceremony instead of having to improvise with a slightly tired, albeit live, interview with perennial Boston favorite Bill Rodgers, who finished fourth, and an announcement that the wheelchair winner would receive $7,500 instead of the expected $2,500.

Peter, who produced this first segment, goes on to review

the taped highlights of the race with the little man in the black-and-white striped shirt, who turns out to be a fitness and running "expert." The word is in quotes because although he may be just that, his commentary lacks insight and incisiveness. Fortunately these elements are well supplied by Peter as he skillfully leads his guest through the start of the race, the men's and women's leaders quickly out front, the travails of Heartbreak Hill, the wheelchair entrants, the last agonized miles, the finish line, and the victors being crowned with the laurel wreath.

After two minutes, thirty seconds of commercials—TWA, the John Hancock Company, the Boston Five (bank), and AT&T (big ticket, all right)—they go live to the Eliot Lounge, where Mike Barnicle in his habitual open-necked blue workshirt garb, talks to a marathon buff from South Boston on the virtues or drawbacks of runners finally receiving substantial prize money. The interview is rambling and inconclusive, and in the control room they start agitating to Mike into his earpiece to speed it up: "Move it, Mike, we're already one minute heavy," i.e., long.

Now comes Andria's piece on Laurie George, in which Laurie's feet do indeed match the rest of her as she approaches the finish line with Andria's voice shouting encouragement.

And Peter winds up the segment joking, "All right, Laurie, you had today off, so we'd like you to be in a little early tomorrow."

To make up time, they start the third segment going right to Mary Richardson without Peter's "throwing" to her, but Mary picks up easily (to an appreciative comment from Susan Sloane: "What a pro") for her interview with a man who five years earlier had had cardiac arrest, followed by a triple bypass, and who has run and finished in the day's race. He wears a Massachusetts General Hospital T-shirt and is accompanied by his cardiovascular unit nurse, who calls her patient "very unique." So "very" in fact, that she says it twice.

Mary then introduces the final sights and sounds of the Marathon played with no voice-over, only music and the natural sounds of cheering crowds; vendors selling balloons, marathon T-shirts, programs; the spectator who has been at the same watching post for thirty-five years; the kids sitting in trees; runners "feeling great," including an eighty-six-year-old man; the starting gun; the cries of joyous anticipation and exhausted misery; and ultimately, at the finish line, of relief and triumph.

Peter does the crossplug, which somehow *did* get finished in time, and then against the video of—what else?—runners running the credits roll: "Producers: Peter Mehegan, Andria Hall, Stella Gould (sights and sounds); Mike Barnicle is a *Boston Globe* columnist; Mary's hair by . . . "

And *Chronicle* circa number 874 is history. Not one for the books, perhaps. Certainly not in a class with Jerry Kirschenbaum's great *Temple of the Golden Buddha*, shot by him in Thailand, narrated by Mike Barnicle, focusing on the struggle and the promise of Southeast Asia after Vietnam, or with Mary Richardson's *Main Streets and Back Roads* from Ireland, a poignant tale of two worlds; bitter violence in the walled northern city of Derry, serenity and enchantment in a tiny hamlet fifteen miles away.

The Boston Marathon is a good workaday program, especially since it is the same workaday, characterized by the high standard of writing, filming, editing, and producing regularly turned out by the *Chronicle*'s thirty-person staff five nights each week.

8

———

Prime Time: Three Specials,
8:00 to 11:00 P.M.

"THE PROGRAM USUALLY seen at this hour will not be shown tonight in order that we may bring you this Channel 5 Special."

The three people, one woman and two men, described in these pages have all been directly concerned with making that announcement necessary. Each of the three has been responsible for first-rate specials that have preempted network prime time.

Lisa Schmid is at work editing a special, a docudrama she has produced and just finished filming. *Secrets* is a true story of a teenaged boy with a drug problem who becomes aware of the devastating effect of his addiction on his family and seeks help to avert tragedy. The dramatized story will run a half-hour, to be followed by Dr. Tim Johnson's interview with the real-life boy and his family.

Schmid estimates that editing *Secrets* will probably take

about four weeks working with editor Jeff Brawer, the best in the business, she believes, who edited the first of her two Emmy-winning programs, *Somerville High*.

In addition to the Emmy, *Somerville High* also won the much more prestigious Peabody award (which the station itself won in 1976) as well as the Associated Press and United Press International awards. "I wouldn't say this normally," Schmid admits, "but I do think it was a great show. I feel very strongly about it."

Somerville High was Lisa Schmid's first documentary for WCVB following her two years as a *Chronicle* field producer. It was conceived in the wake of the Carnegie Commission's report on the abysmal condition of secondary schools in the United States.

After lengthy consultation with Judy Stoia and Charlie Kravetz, who gave her the assignment, Schmid decided to do one typical large urban school. She cast about, considering several other possibilities, then finally chose a ninety-year-old institution in the generally working-class city of Somerville, population 80,000, abutting the larger and more diversified city of Cambridge. "As soon as I walked into that school," she says, "I knew it was the one. The principal, Bill Fasciano, was so honest, open, and straightforward. I could sense from him a spirit about this school even though it was hamstrung with *so* many problems."

"The business of education is in deep trouble," says Natalie Jacobson, who narrated Lisa Schmid and Judy Stoia's script. "For the first time in twenty years, children today are not educated as well as their parents were." The video shifts from a red brick building to a corridor crowded with boys and girls, "victims of the system," elbowing each other as bells ring signaling class changes.

"Academic-wise," says one boy, "school is a drag."

"There are five acres of floor space in this building," Bill Fasciano explains. "And there are nearly twenty-five hundred students, making changes seven times a day, which adds up to a movement of fourteen thousand kids in corridors. Obviously it would take little to send this fragile order into chaos."

To produce this documentary Lisa Schmid spent a total of four weeks at Somerville High, at first getting herself oriented and getting the kids, who had been a bit rambunctious at the outset, accustomed to the TV camera.

What she wanted and what she found were individual students who would reflect the conflicts and frustrations that beset their school community. A kid in trouble: the drug counselor pointed her toward Manny Correia, for whom "life sucks." An enthusiastic eager kid with a solid family background: Lori Mirabella was almost a caricature of the typical gung-ho high school cheerleader. A kid who was really motivated but academically weak: Alan Roycroft, co-captain of the football team, who even in his senior year had trouble reading. A potential dropout: Scott Balleni, who "couldn't hack it." An achiever: Karen Carney was applying to Harvard, Yale, and Dartmouth.

So skillfully did Schmid weave these young protagonists' stories into the fabric of *Somerville High*, so neatly did she introduce other students, teachers, and counselors, each with telling points at issue, that viewers were caught up with their lives, understood what their problems are, and came to care about them and about the special dangers they face.

The Carnegie Commission report gives us dry statistics. It tells us that one-fifth of most school populations are on drugs, that thirty percent of the average graduating class are functional illiterates, that high schools must accept every student who chooses to walk through their doors even if they can't hope to keep up with the norm—the mentally retarded, too many of the non-English-speaking, and those who have already flunked out several times.

But the report doesn't take us into Manny's disjoined home environment as this documentary does, to show us at first hand Manny's despair that his mother just "isn't there for me," that when he can't cope, as he so often cannot, he pops another pill or drinks a fifth of vodka and then can't stop when he wants to stop. It doesn't show us the opposite situation of Lori's strong family life with her thoroughly concerned parents and three supportive older brothers. It cannot re-create the scene with Scott and counselor Robert Sorebella or Sorebella's bittersweet words as he fails to keep the boy in school: "He didn't have a chance. There just wasn't enough guidance. And it's not only the ones you're working with that tear you apart, but those who keep walking by your office and don't come in."

And the teachers. Statistics tell us they are paid salaries more suited to unskilled workers, that the tenure system protects incompetents, that, says Natalie in one of her stand-ups, "the best and the brightest are quitting education to go into more lucrative fields, leaving the nation's classrooms in the hands of those who finished near the bottom of their graduating classes."

But statistics do not show flesh-and-blood teachers, some young and innovative, some wily, salty old hands, hanging in there even though their student load is sometimes overwhelming, their course assignments unsuited to their skills, their trust in the school system shaken. But still they stay, not because they can't go elsewhere but because they are committed.

"The system is only surviving," says one, "because we, the teachers, are subsidizing it. We are picking up the slack."

Nor can any report possibly re-create principal Bill Fasciano's circling the grounds and the building three or four times a day because he thinks his presence is both an encouragement and a deterrent, now stopping to give a word of advice, a rebuke, a reminder, a warning, now breaking the tension by cracking a mild joke with one of his often unruly charges. "I'm a surrogate father, a minister, a psychiatrist, and yes, I guess, above all, I'm also a cop." He smiles cheerfully.

The last segment of *Somerville High* is very upbeat as, in Natalie's narration, "students escape to a world where their energies find expression." Starting with band practice—and a very good high school band it is, too—it goes on to gymnastics, with students executing what looks like a quite tricky pyramid, to a disco dance and to football practice. Here co-captain Alan Roycroft is a leader, in contrast to the earlier bite we had of him painfully reading aloud. "If it wasn't for football," he says, "I wouldn't have went back to high school."

"Did you deliberately make this last part more optimistic?" I ask Lisa Schmid.

"Yes. We felt we had been depressing enough. And even though the educational process was a shambles, there definitely was a strong school spirit that we wanted to show."

I commend a wonderful little scene she got, first with a bunch of boys sitting around a table talking about girls, then another shot of girls talking about boys. "A universal rite of passage," says the narrator.

But what follows—less universal, one hopes—is a touching, disturbing little scene with Joe, who tells us he was fourteen years old when his son was born. "A kid with a kid, they call me." And suddenly in the midst of all the comparatively wholesome good cheer we are brought face to face with teenaged pregnancies, another wrenching problem these adolescents must contend with today.

"Pretty grim," I tell Lisa Schmid. She agrees. "What do you think made the show so successful?"

"No moralizing," she says after a moment. "And I think because you care about the people. The only villain is the system. I wanted those watching the documentary to end up thinking, 'These are good kids. They could be *my* kids. And they deserve a chance.'"

Somerville High catapulted Lisa Schmid into the win column at Channel 5. She was soon recruited to produce *Growing Pains*, the first of what it was hoped would be a long series of hour-long dramas especially written for WCVB under the umbrella title of Metromedia Playhouse.

Bob Bennett was still in-house at the time, running Metromedia Television from Boston, and this innovative program had his strong stamp of approval, though he had one reservation. He wanted it to be even more innovative; he wanted it to be done live. He argued at a meeting I attended that the new series would receive twice as much critical attention if it introduced a fresh idea of live TV drama. He wanted this even though he knew it was rather like reinventing the wheel. In the mid–1950s to early 1960s, when television dramas were at their height, the days of Playhouse 90, Kraft, Goodyear, Alcoa, and others, the days when (if I may inject a personal note) I was writing for these programs, *all* shows were done live. Not until the television industry moved to Hollywood did filmed or video-taped dramatic shows become the norm, and in the changeover some of the first-night excitement of a live, one-time-only, high-risk performance was lost—something that Bob Bennett wanted to recapture.

But he was not to prevail. "There was a great reluctance on the part of many of us, myself included," says Lisa Schmid. "After all, why do people watch live TV? Because it's exciting. An event is exciting—a football game—but something like a play? Instead of having the hype that it's live, think what you can get in the editing room where you can refine, make it better, more artistic, and in fact more interesting."

Growing Pains, a rather depressing story about a father's devotion to his mentally retarded adult daughter and the attendant complications for his new second wife, received generally favorable critical attention and good ratings, auguring well for the continuation of the playhouse idea and Schmid's career as a producer of specials.

By the time Metromedia Playhouse 2 came along, it was Metromedia in name only as the station waited for Hearst to acquire it from Rupert Murdoch. The second play, called *Blind Alleys* and also produced by Schmid, focused on the difficulties and misunderstandings inherent in a racially mixed (Japanese-American) marriage. Whether because of Metromedia's by then only cursory interest or because Cloris Leachman, who played the American wife to Pat Morita's Asian husband, did not quite see eye to eye with the producer's interpretation, the play, which Schmid thinks had more depth and subtlety than *Growing Pains*, still was not a great success. As of this writing, with Metromedia out of WCVB, the playhouse idea is on hold pending a decision by Hearst on whether or not to pursue it.

Schmid, however, had barely time to recover from this taxing assignment before she was plunged into *A Special Peace*, a Vietnam retrospective which she "post-produced." That is, she could not, because of *Blind Alleys*, go to Vietnam with Mike Barnicle actually to shoot it, but she did the script and the editing. She and Barnicle, who got along famously, both won Emmys for it.

Secrets is her fifth special; with her fine track record Lisa Schmid appears firmly entrenched as a documentary/drama producer, a goal which she must always have had in the back of her mind, although it took her some time to realize it. She had an elite if often chaotic precollege education, going first to the exclusive Windsor School, then being kicked out of another school because her boyfriend brought liquor to a prom and with her connivance spiked the fruit punch. "I had a generally bad behavior," she comments, not without a certain satisfaction.

At Boston University she majored in art history, became interested in Chinese foreign policy, and thought *that* was the field she wanted to enter. It wasn't. After getting her master's degree, she opted against further education, trod water for a time working in a gift shop, decided that maybe her career lay in journalism, and managed to finesse her way to a job as a summer replacement at WPRI in Providence. This seemed to be it, so she stayed on for four years as an on-air reporter until she realized she was dead-ended, yet not sufficiently motivated to start the climb upward to ever-larger markets—Detroit to Washington to New York to network. And besides, she was too self-conscious to devote her life to being on-air talent.

About this time the idea of documentaries began to seem attractive, and, ever-resourceful, she got herself hired by a friend doing a documentary on James Michener and spent a year working as assistant producer of the piece in the South Pacific.

That over, she was again at loose ends, so hopped off to China for a spell. Back in the States, she did a stint at Boston's fine Public Broadcasting Station, Channel 2, from whence many of WCVB's top producers have come. There she met Judy Stoia, who during Schmid's subsequent brief stint in New York had moved to Channel 5 and who ultimately invited Schmid to come on board as a freelance producer for the new program called *Chronicle*.

The highly sensitive, intelligent quality of Lisa Schmid's work speaks volumes for her as well as for the medium in which she has finally chosen to demonstrate her considerable talents.

"He knows something about everything," says his boss, Paul La Camera, and then amends that to, "Or rather he knows a lot about a lot of things." Adds his other boss, Judy Stoia, "I'd hate to play Trivial Pursuit with him."

Lisa Schmid

Jerry Kirschenbaum

He divides his time between *Chronicle*, where his title is Senior Producer, and specials, of which he does at least one, usually two, a year. His name is Jerry Kirschenbaum.

His background is unorthodox—"eclectic" is his word for it. His entry-level job in television was as an intern for *Chronicle* at the age of forty. "I was not your basic television ingenue," he comments. To arrive at this unlofty pinnacle he had followed a route so circuitous as to make Lisa Schmid's peregrinations seem positively as-the-crow-flies.

After graduating in journalism from Michigan State University (so far according to Hoyle), he took a couple of short-term jobs, including a very brief stint at the *New York Times* and a job on a weekly newspaper in the Lower East Side of Manhattan, where he grew up (still pretty much on track) before deciding to chuck it all and join the navy (derailed).

This was to be his first long-term post, and it might have been even longer had not the conflict between being an admiral's aide in the sixties in a navy where "they were killing people" and his growing involvement with the anti-Vietnam movement produced an identity crisis. "It wasn't computing very well in my head," he says. So he quit after completing his five-year hitch and went to work for Union Carbide (which today, owing to the tragic Bhopal incident, might compute very badly in his head) as a specialist in ocean technology and underwater engineering, skills which he had acquired along with numerous others during his naval stint.

But at Union Carbide he discovered his growing fascination with business, so again he made a course correction and left Union Carbide to become head of a small "family-owned" oil company. The family, it turns out, was his own; they had bought the company some years earlier but had never really run it. He stayed with this project for a record twelve years, building the company up to 250 employees and making "a lot of money. A *lot!*"

Then, as night follows day, came "your typical New York

Jewish midlife crisis," as Kirschenbaum began to find making money "not relevant."

At this point I dared to ask if he had a family of his own who might reasonably have found the making of money a bit more to the point. "Oh, yes," he said airily, "I had a wife and two sons."

With his oil company gains he bought a sixty-foot boat, a motor sailer commodious enough for him to live on with his wife and boys while it was berthed in Nantucket during the spring and summer, then sailed it to the Bahamas and lived on it for the winter. Having, as he says, written in one form or another all his life, even in the navy, he now began to write full-time, largely for such posh magazines as *Yachting*, *Sail*, and *Wooden Boat*.

The Bahamian retreat was a tiny island of 150 souls, and the entire way of life, sounding more idyllic than it was in fact, finally strained the marriage to the breaking point. With his wife and sons gone back to Nantucket, Kirschenbaum geared up for a fresh spate of basic decisions.

To begin with, he found his writing meaningless and without social value, as it appealed only to a select and comparatively rich segment of the population. But more important, he found writing for print of *any* sort frustrating. "I had things in my eye that I was forcing to come out in words." Where else could these things come out? The needle of the compass began to point toward television. Furthermore, he realized he had been happiest in his career when he was doing something difficult that he could not do alone, but for which he needed a group of talented of co-workers. The needle edged closer. And finally he knew he wanted to "reconnect with life."

Undaunted by the fact that all he knew about television was how to turn the set on and off, he put his boat up for sale in Fort Lauderdale (today he's still paying bills on it), threw a suitcase into his car, and headed for Boston. Why

Boston? Simple: it had to be either the East Coast or the West Coast. He was "not a California head," and no way was he going to live in New York again. His boys were on Nantucket. So, of course, Boston.

Five years of living on a boat, half the time off a remote underpopulated island, had taught Kirschenbaum that he could "manage with very little money," a lesson he believes most people never learn (perhaps because most people know they *can't* manage with very little money). This "weapon" stood him in good stead in Boston, where he soon realized that the four VHF stations, Channels 2, 4, 5, and 7, were not going to avail themselves of his services—at least so they thought and said.

But they had reckoned without Jerry Kirschenbaum's know-how, his well-instructed sense of the world, his resolution, and, more important, his outstanding natural talents.

Determined to make the stations aware of these, he enrolled in the Boston University School of Communications, in itself something of a feat given his age and his unlikely, on paper at least, qualifications. Then, working through a friend of a friend, he managed to wangle a lunch appointment with Bob Bennett even though he had already been turned down for a job at Channel 5, albeit reluctantly, by Phil Balboni.

Bennett, always one to take flyers on interesting though inexperienced people, was both intrigued and puzzled. "There's something about you that tells me I should give you a shot," he told the applicant, "but I'm not sure at what." Kirschenbaum had a suggestion. Through another friend of a friend he had heard that *Chronicle* was in the works, so he proposed himself as an intern for that still-nascent program. Bennett called Balboni, who hadn't thought to offer anything that humble and was happy to oblige.

It was certainly a foot in the door, but a tenuous one.

Kirschenbaum, for all his spartan standard of living, was fast running out of money; he could, he calculated, afford to work for forty days and nights as a grunt who did everything except go for coffee in his new nonpaying position. But forty days, plus a straight A in the course at Boston University, was more than it took for him to sign on for a real job on *Chronicle*, first as an associate producer (the step below field producer), and to wind up where he really wanted to be when the program finally made its mark as senior producer with time off for specials.

How had he done it? How had he made it so fast? What actually did he have to offer?

"I focused," he starts quite simply, then warming to his theme goes on: "Which is something most young people can't do because they haven't lived on the planet long enough. I would much rather hire me at forty than me at twenty-eight. Not that I'm so sage and all-knowing, but I've lived long enough so my tastes are honed. I've had a pretty interesting life, I've read twelve more years of books, seen that many more plays and movies, heard that many more years of concerts and operas, watched that much more TV. And when finally you bring all that extra body of knowledge onto a television piece, it shows."

Does it? I look at one of his hour-long documentaries, and yes, it does indeed show. *The House on Salem Street* is a saga, seen largely through the eyes of one Italian family, of the immigrants who came to Boston at the turn of the century to settle in the North End—a "melting pot" for new hopeful Americans—on Salem Street. It is a story that has been told again and again, especially during the Statue of Liberty centenary, but certainly never more eloquently than in this vivid and poignant production by Jerry Kirschenbaum.

From the opening shots in Italy in the little hamlet of Melito in the south-central province of Avellino from whence came Crescenzio Mostone in 1893, to a set piece ending in the North End in 1986, a sort of curtain call with all the characters standing frozen in place, the script is strong, often hard-hitting, and full of telling nuance. It is also greatly enhanced by the wonderfully haunting musical score, especially the often repeated theme played by recorders, and by Natalie Jacobson's superb performance as the narrator.*

Kirschenbaum has a scorn for documentaries based not on a dramatic line but on facts, coldly transmitted just as facts. Thus in his script the North End in the 1900s was "a neighborhood smaller than Central Park with more people living in it than any place except Calcutta." The year 1893 was not just 1893 but the year Henry Ford built his first car. Crescenzio Mostone got his first job as a railroad roustabout in the year Teddy Roosevelt stormed San Juan Hill.

The "social cycle of immigration" is explained by the fact that "the immigrant who struggled to come to America resented those who came next, especially as each succeeding immigrant was willing to take a lower wage or a job that no one else wanted." In the North End this ingrained resentment—the Irish who came first, for the Jews who followed, the Jews for the Italians who came after—led to "days filled with conflict as language, religion, culture, and custom were pressed into one street already overflowing with the each family's personal struggle. The American melting pot didn't simmer. It boiled."

Photographs from the days before motion pictures are artfully chosen; a shot of an abandoned grocery store, a dusty bottle of Moxie, an eight-cent Panatello cigar, an ancient cash register, a can of La Tourraine tea, and incongruously a painted religious figure—all these stills effectively played

*The reader is surely aware by now that the words Natalie speaks in her narration are written not by her but by the producer of the piece. The reader may not, however, realize that in all of the stand-ups in which the narrator appears on camera on the scene, the words, often quite lengthy bites, must be memorized since no teleprompter is usable on the streets of a city or in the countryside beyond.

against silence—no audio until Natalie comes on camera. "A time capsule," she says, "filled with the artifacts of immigrants, the debris of their history."

And the long life of Crescenzio Mostone, who died at age ninety-two, and his son Liberdati (called Albert), who plays a most important part in the documentary, does indeed span the history of this country in this century; landmark events are fully chronicled. Immigrants, the first rank and file of the beginnings of the labor movement, carrying signs ("Give us a living wage"); World War I, when the many Italian immigrants who were not yet American citizens recrossed the ocean to fight for Italy along with their adopted country; the Russian Revolution, Sacco and Vanzetti, and the fear of anarchism; the 1922 National Origins Act, which cut in half the quotas of immigrants entering the New World; the first jerky moving pictures of "flappers" dancing the Charleston, while Italian children worked in the sculleries of the houses of the rich; the Depression, the rise of Adolf Hitler, the New Deal, Pearl Harbor, World War II.

Each of these periods is recollected by Al Mostone, his family, and his friends, as well as by his Jewish and Irish neighbors who were not his friends. Only on one issue did they all agree; they united to keep the blacks out of the North End, and about this prejudice, promulgated and kept alive by those who were themselves victims of discrimination, producer Kirschenbaum pulls no punches. He makes it unmistakable that the ugly racist reality has hardly disappeared today. Nor does he fail to make a link to the twelve hundred recently arrived Cambodians now living, with little if any welcome, in Revere. "What happened seventy years ago on Salem Street is happening today on Highland Street."

The piece ends where it started in the Italian town of Melito—one would not have it elsewhere—except that as the town was severely damaged by a 1981 earthquake, roofs are gone and no one lives there anymore: "a hidden ruin in a hidden valley." But still there is a connection to Crescenzio Mostone. And the church still stands, its altar exposed to the sky as Natalie walks there and the camera holds there for son Albert Mostone's final sentimental words: "I can still see him on a hill in that town as a boy herding the sheep, but all alone. No man could ask for a better father than he was."

Judy Stoia says about the program, "It was really wonderful. Jerry and I work very well together. He is brilliant in many kinds of programs. He came up with the story line, and we worked together on how it would all fit together, what should be cut and what added. But he really brought it off."

As Kirschenbaum points out, "Writing in television is not just pure writing, it's construction. Writing is only one component. In television a producer is writer, director, editor all combined. It's a kind of weird discipline. That's why you almost never see the words 'written by' in the credits."

But in *The House on Salem Street* you do. You see "Produced and written by Jerry Kirschenbaum." And that is absolutely as it should be.

Clark Booth comes from another part of the forest, or more specifically a different tree in the same forest. Clark is a NewsCenter 5 man—his boss is Phil Balboni, not Paul La Camera—and he is also talent (hence the first-name basis). When he participates in an hour-long special, which he both writes and appears in, his credit line, unlike those of Lisa Schmid and Jerry Kirschenbaum, reads "*Reported* by Clark Booth."

His specials are produced by Dick Amaral, who's in charge of special events in news and with whom he has a symbiotic relationship; he considers him "the smartest man in the whole business, a wizard at putting it all together." About his own title Clark says, "They call me Special Correspondent, which doesn't mean a thing. That plus a half buck will buy you a cup of coffee."

In this capacity, by whatever name, he appears on an average of three times a week on NewsCenter 5 at Six doing background-type pieces, especially anything that involves some link with the past. Thus a sampling of his four-and-a-half-minute spots (a very long time in a television newscast) have covered such subjects as Nazi war crimes, the hundredth anniversary of the Boston Edison Company, the Duchess of Windsor at the time of her death looking back to her days as the woman for whom a king renounced his throne, and Caroline Kennedy at the time of her marriage looking back to her days as a "princess" in the White House. He frequently does thoughtful spots on sports, naturally enough since his early job in television was as weekend sportscaster for WBZ, Channel 4, a speciality he carried, along with his interest in Catholic-related subjects, to Channel 5 when he came there in 1978.

"I like the reflective stuff," he says, "although you often have to sacrifice your own observations to that of the camera, and the camera can't shoot a concept or a theory. Still I don't want to do hard news. I had enough of chasing around covering fires when I was a kid on a newspaper and in my early days in television."

Although he only worked on one newspaper, the *Quincy Patriot Ledger*, and that for a relatively short time, Clark Booth thinks of himself as a print man, a rarity now that television as a communication form has come of age—if not always of wisdom—and has spawned its own talent. The majority of his fellow workers are somewhat younger than Clark, who is forty-eight, and never worked on a newspaper but began their careers either in radio or television.

But print man or no, he is ambivalent, defensive about what he calls newspaper people's "mean-spirited" attitude toward television. (Read any television critic for a glimpse of print's often scornful, patronizing tone toward the younger communication form.) Clark believes that print journalists have never understood how really difficult it is to do a good job in television and that by their hatchet treatment they have tried to discourage good work. Perhaps, he thinks, it's because of envy of what they perceive to be the higher pay of television people.

On the other hand, he believes that the pressure of the dollar does not as pervasively affect newspapers as it does television. The first person to fight for the "soul and independence of TV news" was his hero Edward R. Murrow of CBS. The battle was continued into the sixties by Fred Friendly, also of CBS, but was finally lost when the corporate/business people who run television won the struggle. "For a time," Clark says wistfully, "it looked like those money people were going to be satisfied with their sitcoms, their cartoons, their movies, and the rest of the prime-time fare, and would leave the news alone to be an island of its own. There was even a hope that the rating struggle would not be played out in the news, but as everybody knows, that battle was finally lost."

Certainly, he insists, he doesn't give a damn about ratings, but it disturbs him that good people have to live in fear of them. "Phil Balboni's a guy I have a lot of respect for, and it hurts me that he's under the constant hammer of ratings. You can't be doing something like news and always looking over your shoulder at what's going to play in the ratings."

"Are you suggesting," I ask, "that Phil Balboni or Emily Rooney or Charlie Kravetz are forced to think in terms of 'Shall we play that story prominently because it will help the ratings?'?"

"No, I'm not. This station has been far and away the best— perhaps the best and most sophisticated in the country. But I'm saying a quality newscast is not always the one the public is going to want to see. And as professionals we ought to be able to say, 'These are the stories they *should* see, this is the way we're going to cover them, and to hell with Nielsen or Arbitron or sweep months.' We should be entirely free of all such considerations in the way we present the news. And I can't say we are or that that kind of freedom from pressure exists in our newsroom."

If there are some such constraints in the Newsroom, they have not prevailed in the specials Clark Booth has done for NewsCenter 5. A case in point is his *A Time Remembered*, written and produced for the observance of the fortieth anniversary of the end of World War II (the occasion, it will be recalled, when President Reagan in an ill-considered gesture placed a wreath at the Bitburg Cemetery, where some infamous Nazis were buried).

A Time Remembered is a lucid, finely articulated, absorbing lesson in history, heightened by powerful photography. It is television demonstrating its potential as a teaching instrument. For those who have forgotten or only dimly remember, the Second World War is brought back into sharp focus; those too young to remember cannot help being caught up in this provocative recounting.

"We have risen from the ranks of barbarians," begins Clark Booth, reciting his own words as he stands, looking suitably British in cap and mackintosh, on the plains of Salisbury at Stonehenge. "So when barbarians rise in our times, it is only a reminder that evolution like every other mortal process is imperfect.... Exactly fifty years ago, Adolf Hitler became Chancellor of Germany."

There follows an intricate documentary revolving around a number of fascinating themes neatly woven together. Of primary importance is the "triumph in the intelligence sphere," which details the crucial role played by a British Intelligence unit that succeeded in cracking the German war code. The Nazis' Enigma machine was fiercely ingenious, a magic typewriter that scrambled the alphabet in many millions of ways; its capacities were infinite.

But early in the war a group of British mathematicians in a John Le Carre–like operation called Ultra Secret, Ultra for short, using key bits of captured information pieced together with the "infinities of mathematics," achieved the feat that permitted them to intercept almost every German command of the war, very often before the Nazi commanders in the field themselves knew about them. "With the supreme arrogance that vulgarized every Nazi instinct," says Clark "the German warlords never conceived that their enemies could possibly crack their code."

Not until 1974, some thirty-five years after the fact, was even the existence of Ultra revealed, and today Bletchley Park, the rambling Georgian estate fifty miles north of London where the unit was housed, is still "embraced in a kind of mist," as much information remains under lock and key. During the war, of course, Ultra Secret was just that—so closely guarded that only a very few knew about it (even the king was not among those few), and Winston Churchill was alleged to have said, "I will personally shoot with my own hands any person who compromises the secret of Ultra."

But as Clark points out, knowing what the Germans were going to do was one thing; stopping them from doing it was quite another. Paramount, of course, was the imperative need never to let the enemy know how much was known about their operations. Although there were ways in which Britain could discreetly blunt attacks they knew were coming, there were also times when security demanded they either bait the trap or, far worse, keep the Germans off guard by doing *absolutely nothing*. Was the terrible bombing of Coventry in November 1940 one of these times? Was the city of Coventry knowingly sacrificed on security grounds? "It is likely," says Clark over a video of Number 10 Downing

Clark Booth

Street "there will never be an answer to this agonizing question."

Although the video enhances and illuminates the narration, as it must, much of it is of necessity stock footage of such cornerstones as busy Trafalgar Square with Edward R. Murrow's "extraordinary reporting" on the audio; of Big Ben (inevitably); of Churchill addressing the Canadian Parliament in Ottawa, sarcastically quoting the German boast that in three weeks England would "have her neck wrung like a chicken," and adding with his incomparable nuance, "Some chicken! Some neck!"; of Versailles, "a chilling symbol of abuse and wealth. There the peace treaty of the First World War was forged, there the Germans renounced their folly and set about repeating it. World War II was thus destined."

More arresting are such live pictures as of Clark clambering around the "tattered relic" of France's much-vaunted Maginot Line, "an abject place, as much of a farce as a landmark today as it was as a system of defense."

Scenes, all too familiarly distressing, of the British Expeditionary Force being evacuated from Dunkirk are given new meaning by the documentary's conjecture that perhaps this was not quite the miracle it had been widely proclaimed. There is evidence that Hitler may have frozen five Panzer divisions for "three priceless days," because, with France already destroyed and Russia "festering in his mind," he actually wanted peace with Britain and figured he had a better chance of achieving it if he did not act to destroy her forces, thus stiffening her legendary will.

Yet another thread in *A Time Remembered* chronicles one of the war's most agonizing moments. D-Day, the Allied invasion of Normandy, had been costly but effective. The Germans were on the run and would have been trapped in France but for one failure—the failure of the Allied forces, in particular of Field Marshal Sir Bernard Montgomery, to close the gap to the north in the town of Falaise. Through this hole "too many escaped to fight too many other days." An important impetus was lost. Indeed the immediate consequence would be the Nazis' bloody last-gasp counteroffensive at Bastogne, resulting in the "Allies' last trauma in Europe," the Battle of the Bulge.

But what if the Allies had closed the gap, what if they had finished the German army completely? "Isn't it fair to say that that one stroke would have totally changed the history of our times?" Clark Booth postulates. For instance, the week the gap at Falaise was breached was also the week of the attempted assassination of Hitler. Had that event coincided with the collapse of the German army in France, the revolt against Hitler would certainly have spread. Instead it was "crushed with demonic savagery."

Even more terrible, if possible, is the thought of untold thousands of Jews who would have been spared from wholesale slaughter by an earlier end to the war. So, too, the advance of Russia in the east could have been curbed; postwar Europe might well have been redefined. And finally,

Booth speculates, there would have been no conference at Yalta, where the three great leaders, Churchill, Roosevelt, and Stalin, met, "each with his own capacity to be ruthless," and where decisions potentially disastrous to the future were taken.

In keeping with its news style, *A Time Remembered* is filled—perhaps too much filled—with Clark Booth interviewing people concerned with and knowledgeable about World War II. By far the most successful of these is William L. Shirer, author of *The Rise and Fall of the Third Reich*, among other important histories, who appears frequently in this documentary. Now eighty-two years old, looking pink and white with his beard and long wispy hair, he speaks with straightforward, unpretentious clarity about a momentous epoch in our history.

"To know Clark one must know *A Time Remembered*," says his producer and friend Dick Amaral.

"I don't know of any other station in the country," says Clark, "that would have let two cranky old guys like Dick and me, plus our cameraman, Jake O'Callahan, travel all around France, Germany, Belgium, and England, recalling all these moments of World War II. It was great."

"So too is the result," I tell him.

"We tried to do something in the Bill Moyers style, but of course we don't have his staff. And we certainly can't do a documentary like that every other week. We are, after all, a local television news station. We are not Public Broadcasting."

I think of these three documentaries, chosen, it must be said, because all three are examples of WCVB at its best, which certainly puts it on a par with Public Broadcasting. I say as much to Clark.

"Yes," he concedes and adds with his sardonic tough-guy grin, "you might say we're the best of a bad lot."

9

Weekend

THE CONTRAST BETWEEN weekday and weekend offerings on television is, to put it charitably, preposterous. After the eleven o'clock news comes to an end on Friday night, it is almost as if the viewer were stepping from a comparatively lively, populated continent into a desert with only a few widely scattered oases.

At WCVB, for instance, as opposed to seven weekday hours of local programming, five live and two taped, Saturday has but two hours, the six and eleven o'clock news (sometimes even one of these half-hours is preempted), plus a sentimental favorite, a taped hour show that has been running continuously for twenty-eight years on Channel 5's air and is devoted to a sport endemic only to parts of New England and the Maritime Provinces, called candlepin bowling. This weekend drought exists throughout the industry both local and network, with the exception of sports spectaculars that usually take up the part of Saturday daytime that is not stacked end to end with cartoons for the little ones.

Why should this be so? Granted that Americans, who today have more leisure than ever before, are likely to be off in great numbers feverishly jogging or playing tennis or volleyball, skiing in winter, swimming or boating in summer, there is still a far larger potential daytime *weekend* audience than on any given workday. So why would this not be an opportune time for a good local station like WCVB to take the lead in offering more rather than far less creative programming, even to floating a fresh experimental idea or two?

In fairness I must quickly point out that Sunday, as distinct from Saturday, is quite another matter. But before moving on to consider that more fertile day, I feel obliged to say a few words on behalf of *Candlepin Bowling* and its estimable host, Don Gillis. It may be recalled that Don was mentioned earlier as a top talent from the old *Herald Traveller*-WHDH days whom Leo Beranek and Bob Bennett managed to entice into the BBI fold. Widely looked upon as the dean of Boston sportscasters and as such much admired, he is semiretired now, a charming, wryly humorous man who confines his reportorial activities to a few specials and the not-very-taxing bowling show. And while I'm at it, candlepin differs from regular bowling in that a small grapefruit-sized ball is used and the pins, while not shaped like any candle I have ever seen, are still different from those used in ordinary big-ball, thumb-and-finger-in-the-hole bowling.

Not long ago on a Monday morning I found myself sitting in the CVB sound truck parked outside the Fairway Bowling emporium in suburban Natick, watching Producer Phil Rubin direct the taping of the *Candlepin Bowling* show, which would air twelve days hence on a Saturday at 12:30 P.M. Three cameras provide the video for these contests between two bowlers, usually a local champion from some town in the viewing area, and a challenger. Camera 1 is positioned midway down the alley to catch the bowler (neatly clad in a red polo shirt bearing the emblem *Channel 5,*

Candlepin Bowling) about to roll the ball; Camera 2 is mounted on a platform to show the bowler from behind as he or she releases the ball; and Camera 3 is on a close-up of the pins.

The audience is very loyal indeed and large, you may be sure, to keep the show running even on a Saturday afternoon for so long. Between strings Don Gillis mentions the birthday of one of the true believers, who has "rarely missed a program in the show's twenty-*six* years." His error must have been pointed out to him because this genial man, who has been with *Candlepin* since its inception, quickly corrects it. "Did I say twenty-six? I'm wrong, of course. It's twenty-eight years. It just *seems* like twenty-six."

After three strings Don gives out the prize money and the obligatory statuettes, and then he and the crew take a fifteen-minute break before starting all over again to tape the next show—they do three at a crack—and I have a few moments to talk with him.

There being no more I want to know about candlepin bowling, I steer the conversation around to baseball, a fruitful subject since it prompts Gillis to reminisce about the times in the early 1950s when he had been the reporter assigned to stay at home when the Red Sox were on the road or, if they got rained out, to provide the stations in their network with a substitute game. (This, to be sure, was in radio, not television.) "So," he recalls, "it would be just myself and a telegrapher from Western Union sitting in the studio re-creating a game being played, let's say, in New York. In these primitive first days you could actually hear the Morse code coming in, da-da-da-da-dee-dee. The telegrapher would interpret the signal, type it, then put in front of me something like—we'll say that the Yankees were playing Detroit—'Kaline up.' I would know that Vic Raschi was pitching for New York and Yogi Berra was catching. The next thing that would come across would be 'S1 C'—Strike One

Called, and then next would be 'B1, B2,' and then there would be simply 'Out. Kaline flied right.' So what you'd try to do with those bare facts was to play with them a little bit. You'd say, 'Raschi leans in for the sign. [Voice rising a little.] Here's the two-one pitch on the way. . . . Swung on! [Excitement level getting higher.] There's a drive deep to right [Fever pitch]. Hank Bauer going back—back—back. Aa-nn-dd—he—TAKES IT!"

And so to Sunday, pausing briefly at the cusp, as it were, to look in on *The Great Entertainment*, a late-night offering of films from the Hollywood glamour era of the forties and fifties. The program, which dates back to the Bennett days, makes a palpable effort to come up with something a bit different from the usual late, late show formula. It is dressed up with its own set—a theater marquee—and with its host, Frank Avruch, who appears in evening clothes to set the movie up and fill in between the endless commercials with nice behind-the-scenes tidbits and updates on the stars of thirty-odd years ago. *The Great Entertainment* starts at 11:30 on Saturday and runs usually until 2:00 A.M. and then again, with a different film, on Sunday night.

If Frank Avruch puts the Channel 5 faithfuls to sleep on a Saturday night, he also joins them on Sunday morning for, as he puts it, their second cup of coffee with a program called *Sunday Best*, which is in fact just that, a montage of the highlights of the preceding week's *Good Day!*, *Chronicle*, specials, or special news features.

Dressed casually in an open-necked sports shirt this time, Frank opens the Sunday show at 9:00 with the first live news and weather of the day. In order to put the program together and to write all the intros and "outros," he and his assistant talk to the various producers and reporters involved in the pertinent segments to get their insight on the particular parts chosen for *Sunday Best*—usually there are about six or seven pieces dealt with during the hour.

Don Gillis   Marjorie Arons-Barron

A more significant offering is a panel show taped on Friday for showing on Sunday at 11:00 A.M. *Five on Five* features four well-qualified commentators—Doris Kearns Goodwin, political scientist and historian, and Hubie Jones, social scientist, loosely defined as the two liberals, with John Collins, former mayor of Boston, and columnist Avi Nelson the conservatives—grappling with some of the past week's most pressing and newsworthy questions, usually two of national interest and one local. Peter Mehegan is the show's adroit moderator.

Five on Five is called a public affairs program, a much-used, often deceptive and even self-serving term. By most definitions public affairs is any program that has as its primary objective edifying rather than simply entertaining the public. Realistically one might also note that if the given program manages to provide a bit of entertainment, and thereby to make a bit more money, fair enough, so long as the underlying purpose is not obfuscated. Joseph Heston, executive producer/programming, who oversees much of the weekend, as well as *Good Day!*, thinks of a public affairs program as one that discusses issues of public importance and therefore has a license not to come in first in the ratings. To which I would add, it had better come in at least second and not lose too much money.

Five on Five qualifies on all counts; it edifies, it does not win its time slot, it loses money but not too much, and it entertains, as the four panelists put on a lively show. There are those who think that in their enthusiasm they constantly interrupt each other, but even if they do, it is important to remember that this, like similar programs, is aired as taped— no editing, no redoing for glitches or smoothing over the rough spots likely to occur when bright people of differing views meet head to head. In fact, they are all good friends, and most of them have been with the show for at least five of its eight years on the air.

They play to an audience of between 85,000 and 100,000, large but certainly not enormous by television standards. But, says Doris Kearns Goodwin, it is an intensely loyal audience. "You walk down the streets and people really know who you are. Not in the sense of being a celebrity, but because they want to talk about the issues you have just expressed. After some of my other television experiences, people commented about how I looked. After *Five on Five* they comment about what I think." No question about it, the show is an opinion maker, whether they are discussing airline safety, seat belts, birth control education in public schools, teachers' strikes, or the Iran arms deal. The show is produced by Marjorie Arons-Barron, who holds the important job of director of editorials, a combination of effort which she says is quite logical since the subjects she chooses for *Five on Five* often feed off ones she has done editorials on during the week.

It will be remembered that BBI in its original proposal to acquire Channel 5 committed itself to editorializing on a regular basis at a time when most stations didn't have editorials at all, and that Harvard professor Oscar Handlin was WCVB's first distinguished chairman of the editorial board. Now, as then, that board consists of nine members who meet each Tuesday and reach, according to Arons-Barron, "that ineffable something called consensus" in choosing topics.

Channel 5 editorials are omnipresent; five different ones every week, read by either Jim Coppersmith or Marjorie Arons-Barron, are aired four times each day—that is, after the *Eyeopener*, after the *Midday*, during *NewsCenter 5 at Six*, and for insomniacs who are gluttons for punishment at 3:40 A.M. At the weekend they are repeated. The editorials run a minute to a minute and a half and seem longer, perhaps because they are worthy but lackluster, rather like a high school principal talking in assembly to the student body.

On the other hand, editorials, although they could use a little more imaginative presentation, have been a staunch presence. When Metromedia acquired it, WCVB was the only station in the consortium to have editorials, a circumstance that might have been a cause for apprehension on Arons-Barron's part. But Bob Bennett saw it as an opportunity and made sure that she was sent around to the other stations to initiate editorial programs from scratch, a process she greatly enjoyed. She felt she was acting as a sort of missionary for the whole process.

Another aspect of public affairs is community service, constantly alluded to along with "quality programming" in boiler-plate statements about a station's lofty aims. That is not to say community service is not important, because it is. It provides access to minorities and becomes their means of being heard and having their problems aired. All stations have someone on staff who is concerned with community relations, but at Channel 5 that person is at the vice-presidential level, meaning that she reports directly to Jim Coppersmith, although she looks on Paul La Camera, as do so many others at CVB, as her mentor. Donna Latson-Gitten, who has worked for all three of Boston's major stations, considers her job at Channel 5 to be many-pronged. Most visibly, she is in charge of the public service campaign, the already mentioned, highly successful *World of Difference* campaign against prejudice and discrimination, which ran to great and good effect for two years. For this WCVB won the Gabriel Award "for outstanding achievement by a television station, defined as consistent quality in all programming and a total commitment to community service." Begun in the fall of 1986 was the new *Don't Be Pushed* campaign aimed at youthful drug abusers.

Donna Gitten's other duties include handling all *pro bono* notes of community interest broadcast by the station. She is also a member of the editorial board and, perhaps most important, she oversees all community specials, such as the recent one on South Africa and also *Straight Talk: Gays in Boston*, and is responsible for two weekly half-hour public affairs shows, *Aqui* and *City Line*, targeted for particular audiences.

There was a time when the FCC regulations demanded that at least one time period in weekly programming be directed toward such minority-oriented programs. But now that deregulation has erased even that minimal obligation, many stations have entirely sloughed off their targeted programs. Some managers argue, perhaps with reason, that because their stations are now doing a better job of integrating minority affairs into the whole range of their programming, special minority programs are no longer necessary. While conceding the justification of this argument, Paul La Camera continues to oversee *Aqui* and *City Line*, both airing on

Donna Latson-Gitten   Arthur Miller

Sunday, a commitment that, along with their frequent community specials, makes Channel 5's public service programming far above the average for the country at large.

Aqui, produced entirely by Hispanics in Spanish with English subtitles, concerns itself with problems facing the "Latinos," as they call themselves. Recently, for instance, the program was devoted to the nagging question of high school dropouts—more common among Hispanics than any other minority. Forty-three percent of a class entering in 1981 failed to graduate in 1985, a startling and discouraging statistic. To offset this, a newly instituted bilingual program promises to help ameliorate the situation, as attested to by interviews with several of the young students themselves. *Aqui*'s co-hosts are Joe Masso and Mayra Rodriguez-Howard; the show regularly plays to an audience of some 25,000 people.

City Line is concerned with questions that have to do with living in the city. As Karl Nurse, executive producer/community programming, points out, "The minute you start discussing urban problems, your by-product is going to be mainly black programming in one way or another." Still, the access is there for other inner-city dwellers, especially since *City Line* does not only concentrate on frustrating problems but sometimes addresses a compelling and cheerful subject such as the recent "Jazz World in Boston" as seen through the eyes of prominent black musicians, a black disk jockey, an agent, an entrepreneur, a photographer, and a variety of jazz buffs both black and white.

City Line's host is Ron Allen, a regular news reporter, and its producer, who also conducts most of the interviews, is Karen Holmes. The show is varied and lively and has an audience of between 60,000 and 75,000 viewers.

Onward, then, to Sunday evening and the durable *Miller's Court*, the longest non-news program, after *Good Day!*, still seen on WCVB's air. Arthur Miller, a professor at the Harvard Law School, relishes his role as the program's progenitor and title character because, as he points out without a trace of false modesty, "I am animated and dramatic in the classroom. I try to be interactive so that nobody falls asleep. There's always been a cult about my teaching." Thus, since he often has visitors who come to hear him perform, he was not surprised to see two strangers sitting at the back of his class on a day nine years ago.

It happened on that particular morning that he was teaching something "incredibly complicated" in his first-year procedure class, and it may have crossed his mind to wonder what the two men at the back were making of it all. Right after class they came up and introduced themselves: Bob Bennett and Bill Pourvu. Was he free for lunch? He was. At lunch Bob Bennett said to him in words he has never forgotten, "You know, I haven't the foggiest idea what you were talking about. But there was something going on in that classroom. And I wonder if there isn't a way of translating that into television."

The result, first called *Right or Wrong* but promptly changed, is a tribute to Bob Bennett's creative, fertile imagination, his readiness to take chances, and BBI's willingness to encourage so many of his novel, untried ideas. And perhaps the fact that *Miller's Court* in its first two years was far more free-flowing—mostly Miller rapping with a studio audience—than it is in today's more structured and slightly glitzy versions, speaks to the difference between BBI and the subsequent Metromedia/Hearst regimes.

Executive Producer Joe Heston calls the current *Miller's Court* "a contrived reality," a label that aptly expresses the format. The lawyers are real lawyers, and the jury is real, although the people are not chosen at random the way a regular jury would be since several are selected each week to ensure differing opinions on whatever is at issue, with others coming from the studio audience. The witnesses, however, are actors, and they open the program with a little minute-and-a-half dramatization of the action that results in the forthcoming "trial." For example, a mother and her teenage son are having breakfast when a furious man forces his way in accompanied by a young girl and accuses the son of having gotten his daughter pregnant, which, it develops, he had. Question: Should the boy's family be held responsible?

After this so-called vignette there is no script, so to a certain extent the cast still wings it, but the show is not aired as taped the way it was in the good old days. Now it goes through post-production, meaning that it is edited, and somehow this process makes it all seem rather pat. The real lawyers examine the witnesses, and Arthur Miller interprets and moves the scene along toward his final climactic segment with the jury, an "interaction" which he says closely resembles his style of teaching. The jury then goes off to consider their verdict during a commercial break.

And yes, the boy's family *is* held responsible.

The news at six and eleven on Saturday and Sunday evenings follows the routine with which we are now familiar, but with a difference. Somehow I had expected that news on the weekend would closely resemble the news at 5:30 A.M. in that both programs are out of the mainstream newscasts, and both are prepared and produced without benefit of top-dog staff, which makes for a heady sense of freedom and independence. At 5:30 this feeling is exhilarating; at that ghostly early-morning hour the *esprit de corps* is as high as the discipline is strong. Not so the weekend; too often Saturday and Sunday news programs gave the impression that they were only on the air because they were *scheduled* to be there, not because they had anything important to broadcast.

Recently, as I sat in on preparations for a Sunday-night six o'clock news program, I was struck with the fact that although everyone was certainly doing his or her job with efficiency and dispatch, the atmosphere was casual almost to the point of indifference. Almost. Certainly the pre-air-time tension which is manifest just before every other news program was conspicuously absent on this particular Sunday evening. So much so that Jack Harper, then anchor of the show and an extremely well-liked journalist, commented half apologetically to me as they all—crew, reporters, anchors, and producers—stood around gaping at a football game, about this being an unusual evening. Rarely were they so relaxed and easygoing just before a broadcast. But in fact something else was going on that evening of which I was not then aware; it could be described as whistling in the dark.

Not surprisingly the trouble, as I was soon to discover,

had to do with ratings. Channel 5's weekend news had fallen into what Coppersmith describes as "serious second" to Channel 4, meaning not so far above third-place Channel 7.

Meanwhile other wheels were turning. Even on weekdays the six o'clock news was not exactly thriving. While frequently tied with Channel 4 for first place, it almost never actually won the time slot and often was in second—albeit not "serious" second place. One possible reason for the stubborn gap was that Channel 4 had for some time had a successful early-evening news show running at 5:30 which if nothing else provided that station with a strong lead-in to its six o'clock. Through the years Channel 5 had mostly managed to surmount this lead-in, although it often considered but then usually dropped the idea of running a similar program at five.

Matters came to a head, however, when a major and much-desired new talent suddenly became available. Jay Schadler, an ABC national correspondent who covered much of the country but was based in Boston, decided he had had enough of traveling over half the year and being away so much from his family, so he chose to throw his lot in with a local station. Having looked into many of ABC's affiliates in the course of his widespread assignments, he considered that "Chicago perhaps was a little stronger politically but that Boston across the board had the best broadcast journalism in the country."

Naturally Phil Balboni and Jim Coppersmith jumped on his bandwagon and persuaded him that WCVB was where he belonged. He agreed, although with certain conditions. There was some question as to exactly where to put him since he had made it clear that he was not interested in quitting the network just to be a reporter even in this best local station. He would only come as an anchor. This led WCVB's management once again to dust off and consider the idea of a five o'clock news program for Schadler to anchor, but other possibilities for that time slot were looming (for example, reruns of the *Bill Cosby Show* will become available in late 1987). Even more important, the parlous condition of the weekend news strongly suggested putting Schadler in there to shore things up.

It so happened that the very Sunday I was observing the six o'clock news was the day Jack Harper had been called to Phil Balboni's house to be informed that although he would of course be kept on as the valued reporter they all knew him to be, he was going to be replaced as anchor. A few weeks earlier Harper's co-anchor, Krista Bradford, never one of the brightest lights in CVB's firmament, had been told she would be let go; her replacement, Dawn Fratangelo, was due to arrive from San Diego in December.

So a strong second team was in the wings waiting to go on, and inevitably this led to a spate of rumors in the local press that the second team was in fact being lined up to replace the first team of Natalie Jacobson and Chet Curtis, who were in the fifth year of their five-year contract.

Such speculation was vigorously denied by Balboni—("Our intention is that Chet and Natalie continue to anchor the news together for as long as we can see into the future") and by Coppersmith ("I hope with all my heart we can sit down and negotiate another five years"). Each man, however, qualified his denials ever so slightly. "Having a strong weekend team," said Balboni, "is good insurance if ever something unforeseen should happen to our main anchor team." And Coppersmith: "It doesn't hurt to have a strong bench. You never know when you might have to look down there and send someone into the game."

To these and other, mildly forked conjectures, Chet Curtis, who more than Natalie Jacobson seemed to be the principal target (possibly because, since Dawn Fratangelo had not yet arrived, Jay Schadler was perceived as the stronger of the two new weekend anchors), responded with his characteristic grace and equanimity. "I have no illusions about this job," he said. "It's not civil service; it's not a lifetime job, and so I'm not concerned about being blown out of here. I think I do a good job, but I could be a reporter again too. ... If I were told next week that I was no longer going to do the six and eleven, it would be a blow to my ego, but I understand the nature of the business and I would not slash my wrists."

At times like this a television station can be disheartening. Here we have a superior anchor team whose value to the station is immeasurable, somewhat compromised because of ratings. And, make no mistake about it, ratings are, at best, a questionable form of measuring success or failure. At worst they may be a sword of Damocles hanging over the heads of highly professional people who must without question accept what they dictate as "the nature of the business."

Yet as far as the weekend news is concerned, Channel 5 viewers will probably benefit from this rash of attention to what may well have been a flawed product, conspicuously lacking a sense of mission.

Sign-off

CAN TELEVISION ANY longer be looked on as a public trust, or is it now only a vast moneymaking business?

That question, asked at the start of this book, must now be addressed. But first it must be qualified. "Public trust" is a high-sounding phrase that is in fact somewhat ambiguous, so it might be more to the point to ask the question another way. Is television, meaning the combination of network and local affiliates, doing as good a job as it should be in entertaining, informing, and enlightening its viewers?

The answer is, regretfully, no. Blame for this rests in large part with the three networks that dominate the daily schedule of even their most independent-minded affiliates, and far too often fill their airways with, to put it charitably, banalities. Nor does the FCC, created with public funds to protect the people's interest, come close to holding the industry even to minimum broadcast standards by demanding that both stations and networks devote a prescribed number of hours per week to quality programming.

The answer to the second part of that question is yes. Making large amounts of money is indeed what animates the television industry. The money, in fact, is enormous. Newspaper and magazine profits pale beside it.

As long as large profits remain the primary objective, commercial television will never quite be able to fulfill its potential. If thoughtful, provocative programming and enlightened presentations of the news can prosper only if they make money, the need to compromise can put a station's integrity at risk.

This is not as it should be. Public libraries are also a public trust. They would be violating that trust if they offered their readers nothing but a wide selection of lurid romances and formula mysteries, and rarely a biography, modern history, children's tale, or serious novel. But those mysteries and romances are in fact the equivalent of what much of television offers its viewers. The degree to which any local station deviates from that fare is the degree to which it may be considered to be truly serving the public interest—even if it succeeds in making money in doing so.

I must make clear at once that when I use the word *television*, I do not mean public television, which is of course a very different proposition. PBS stations have only to worry about not losing money—a very substantial worry, to be sure, but one which allows them to operate with quite a different set of values. Theirs is not the stuff of sitcoms and game shows, but rather of substance or (to quote Judy Stoia again) of the eat-your-vegetables kind of programming.

To the so-called intellectuals or putative eggheads, among whom snobbery about television in general is the rule, Boston's PBS, Channel 2, is still sacrosanct. "Local news on Channel 5? When does that come on?" . . . "Oh, but I couldn't watch at that hour. And miss *MacNeil-Lehrer*?" Or

"I don't even bother to take a TV to the Vineyard because I can't get Channel 2 there."

It is true, however, that the closer Channel 5 comes to doing the sort of shows that Channel 2 does, the more quality programs it in fact produces. Furthermore, as we have seen, many of Channel 5's most gifted staff and talent come from Channel 2; Judy Stoia, for one—a considerable plus for any station—not only came herself but brought a lot of the people who now work on *Chronicle* with her.

Still, without denying the fine, edifying influence of all our Channel 2s, I now consider a rhetorical choice. If some almighty power were to decree we could have only one kind of television—public (government- and viewer-supported) or commercial (mercantile-supported)—I would have to opt for commercial. I know, I know, all those soaps, all the violence, and that junk.

Even so, the value of commercial television is in its very nonelitism. With true Jeffersonian/Jacksonian democracy it reaches everyone, a powerful magnet that attracts a vast segment, in fact the majority, of our population. Given its remarkable influence, the one thing television must never do is to play to the lowest common denominator. Yet unfortunately the industry is prone to do just that. Those stations that steadfastly resist this temptation are what this book is about.

WCVB, Channel 5, is an exemplar. While not alone in its determination to enlighten rather than pander to the public, its staff has a unity of purpose that other local stations would do well to follow. Basically this collegiality is rooted in the BBI days; it suffered during the Metromedia reign and would, I believe, have been strongly rekindled if Phil Balboni, Paul La Camera, Jim Coppersmith, et al., had prevailed in their desire to return the station to local *and* to employee ownership. But now what of Hearst?

The auguries are favorable. On the day their purchase of

CVB became a fact, Hearst Broadcasting took a full-page ad in the *Boston Globe* and in every other newspaper in the Channel 5 viewing area. It read:

IT'S OFFICIAL. WCVB-TV CHANNEL 5 IN BOSTON IS
NOW A PART OF HEARST BROADCASTING

WELCOME Richard Albert, Anne Alden, Rodney Allen . . .

And there followed the full name—no Chets or Jims or Judys—of every single employee, all 356 of them, in alphabetical order.

A gesture, to be sure, but certainly a start on the right foot. It was followed by other heartening gestures to staff and community, culminating in a spectacular party, a "celebration of WCVB joining Hearst." Held in Symphony Hall for some seven hundred guests, including, in addition to local luminaries, such notables as Senators Edward Kennedy and John Kerry, and ABC stars Barbara Walters and Ted Koppel. Governor Michael Dukakis was present; his father-in-law, Harry Ellis Dickson, conducted the Boston Pops Orchestra, and Itzhak Perlman gave an exceptionally stirring performance. John Kluge, billionaire head of Metromedia who sold WCVB down the river, was there to see how differently he might have behaved, as was Bob Bennett, full of warm smiles and, as always, much beloved.

The party, marked on all sides by thoughtful planning and good taste, had what one impressed guest called "real panache." *Boston* magazine thought so too and gave it their "Party of the Year" award.

Pleasant and reassuring signs notwithstanding, Hearst is still a mammoth corporation, with 135 different enterprises and more than 12,000 employees. As such it cannot help being a bit removed as far as WCVB is concerned.

Much has been said and written by Hearst Corporation

President and Chief Executive Officer Frank A. Bennack, Jr., about his company's commitment to excellence, his pride in WCVB's honored and well-deserved national reputation, his determination to continue to offer the finest in local programming and community service.

Attempting to get some concrete answers, I posed a few questions directly to John Conomikes, Bennack's vice president and general manager of broadcasting, and the man to whom Jim Coppersmith reports.

I told him quite frankly that because CVB had been pretty well buffeted about by the circumstance of three owners in fourteen years, I felt that some assessment of the depth of Hearst's commitment to the ideals of this station was in order.

Citing what is indeed the benchmark of a topnotch station, Conomikes, a long-time Hearst officer, pointed out that his company had known at the time of its purchase that WCVB did more local programming than any other station in the country—this was one of the features that made it so great. "Naturally we were going to do nothing whatsoever to harm this very successful operation."

I was reminded of my talk with Phil Balboni way back on the night the story first broke, when he pointed out to me that, having paid a stupendous sum for what was certainly one of the biggest money-making stations in the country, Hearst would hardly want to do anything to change what they had bought.

"At the time we acquired CVB," Conomikes was saying, "a broadcaster from another group called up to congratulate us on having bought such a wonderful station. 'You know,' he told me, 'you could improve their profitability by several million dollars simply by cutting back substantially on the staff. You don't need all those people to run the station.' Our answer was, 'Maybe, but that's not why we bought the station. We bought the station for what it is and how it has performed. Our intention is certainly not to change the composition of CVB and the wonderful contribution they make to the broadcasting industry.' And time will prove that we mean what we say." Time indeed has.

I put another litmus test to him, asking his view of *Chronicle*, often referred to on these pages as symbolic of what WCVB stands for. Without hesitation Conomikes replied, "*Chronicle* is the most splendidly locally produced Monday-to-Friday show in the business, and it sets us apart from what anyone else is doing."

Trying to place myself in the corporate level, bottom-line mode, I asked about the status of *Chronicle* in the marketplace. How did he think it did financially with game shows, *Wheel of Fortune* and *Jeopardy*, the highest rated syndicated programs in the country stacked against it?

"We could perhaps get a bigger audience with *Wheel of Fortune*," he said, "but that's not what it's always about. So I'll tell you that if someone came to me and said, 'Hey, you can have *Wheel of Fortune*. It's yours; we'll give it to you at a very inexpensive price, but it's got to go into *Chronicle*'s time period and *Chronicle* has to go off the air,' we would stay with *Chronicle*. Because though of course we're there to deliver as large an audience as we can, we want to do it with the very best program we can put on the air."

Given this positive, if generalized, view, I think it is fair for me to conclude that although I may not see inherent in Hearst the ability, imagination or even desire to have *created* the WCVB that evolved in 1972 under the fortuitous combination of BBI and Bob Bennett, what I do indeed see in Hearst is a solid appreciation of what their predecessors wrought and a determination to continue down that same path and even to widen its parameters along the way.

Meanwhile, on the home front the response to their current owners is so enthusiastic as to be positively euphoric, especially on the part of Jim Coppersmith, who has the most direct dealings with them. He and Conomikes have much in common; both long-time savvy television men whose tough-minded realism is sprinkled with idealism, they get along like blood brothers. But for Frank Bennack, Coppersmith reserves very special praise. "A great leader, he is the spirit of the Hearst company," says WCVB's general manager, recalling with particular pleasure Bennack's endearing habit of simply picking up the phone for no stated reason and calling with words of encouragement ("You and your staff are a credit to us").

"Whenever he does that, it's like Christmas," glows Coppersmith. Then, characteristically down to earth, he further notes that under Hearst the employee benefits are more far-reaching, progressive, and sophisticated than offered by either of the previous owners.

Paul La Camera, number two in the ruling triumvirate, while an optimist by nature, is genuinely enthusiastic about the future of programming under Hearst. "They have been magnificent," he says. And the third man in the triumvirate, Phil Balboni, the one most involved with trying to buy CVB before Hearst did, says without equivocation, "I don't think my dreams have in any way been snuffed out by our inability to acquire the station. I think in Hearst we have a very compassionate and understanding ownership."

So perhaps I am alone in looking back now and again with a touch of wistfulness to that unrealized dream of local ownership and employee profit sharing. Certainly without at all disparaging Hearst, it can still be argued that the probability of arriving at a bottom-line solution is greater in any large corporation than it would be with a local owner right on the premises taking the pulse and making the day-to-day decisions. But realistically, the wherewithal to implement such decisions is certainly more readily available to Hearst than it would be to a local owner. And finally, since it is clearly in the nature of American enterprise that huge corporations ultimately take over small, locally owned companies, to complain about such an outcome is like complaining about the nature of evolution.

Ratings, a fact of TV life, seem to produce a kind of unreality—an Alice in Wonderland mist that often envelopes this industry, called quite literally *broad*casting.*

Where else but in television would the numbers, the sheer bulk of the viewers reached by one program or another on a given night, be so overwhelming? For a publisher to be told that one of his books is a failure because it has reached *only* 4.5 million people would be farcical. Few best sellers ever reach that many people; certainly none has ever done so on a single night.

To put the number of viewers in some perspective, I have arrived, by my own method but using impeccable sources, at the figure 115,875,000 as the number of people who watched the Super Bowl in 1982 when that contest won the highest rating ever recorded for a sporting event. The figure 115,875,000 is close to half the population of the United States.

On the other hand, we were repeatedly told at the time of Prince Andrew's wedding to Sarah Ferguson that the ceremony was watched by 300 million people throughout the world. That figure is almost three times the total population of the United Kingdom, and the hour (5:30 A.M.) certainly precluded a very large audience in either North or South America. Furthermore, we were often reminded that that figure 300 million was paltry compared with the 750 million that watched Prince Charles and Lady Di through their paces five years earlier. Incredible! I just plain do not believe that

---

*Someone in my hearing recently used the word *narrowcasting*—an official though little-used term referring to very small target audiences, i.e., young males between the ages of thirteen and fifteen interested in lacrosse.

three-quarters of a *billion* people watching any wedding, no matter how gloriously ceremonial, can honestly be substantiated.

Moreover, I think that the entire system of "audience estimates" as practiced in this country by two companies, Arbitron and Nielsen, is at best inexact and at worst misleading. In this view I am supported by no less an authority than William Ruben, vice-president for research at NBC, who was quoted in the *Wall Street Journal* as saying that TV is the only industry he knew of that lets a "research methodology dictate its behavior."

Exactly what is the research methodology? There are basically two ways to measure viewer preference: diary keepers and meters. A meter, about the size of a pack of cigarettes, is attached to the back of each TV set in a given household; it clamps onto a wire leading to a portable computer tucked away in a closet where it cannot be tampered with. As soon as a TV set is turned on, it starts an electronic tape that records what channel has been turned on or changed and stores that information onto the portable computer. These data are then retrieved at the end of a twenty-four-hour period; the stations can call early each morning to get preliminary ratings of the previous day's programs, an immediacy they find indispensable. In the afternoon they receive the final printout. Such information is undoubtedly accurate but expensive to acquire and is not really weighted, or, in the words of the *Wall Street Journal*, it only "passively measures channel changes without regard to who is watching."

Diary keepers, of course, are people, always a plus factor. They are supposed to write in little books—seven-day diaries—what station they are watching whenever their set is turned on or whenever they change channels. The system is obviously fallible; the keepers forget or are lazy (not surprisingly, since to prevent any suspicion that the rating services are trying to "buy" them, they receive the munificent sum of fifty cents per week for their trouble), their hand-writing is usually illegible, and they often record what they think they *should have* been watching rather than what, if anything, they actually were watching.

The diary keepers' chief value is that they provide the demographics engendered by zip codes and U.S. Census Bureau statistics. The audience survey companies weight their samplings of diarists to appropriately include high- or middle- or low-income families and varying ethnic back-grounds. No household has both a diary keeper and a meter; the information each generates must therefore be juggled by the station, using whichever comes out best, to arrive at the ever-vital "numbers."

In sum, then, if I am not oversimplifying, meters produce accurate information but not a clue to who is providing it, and diary keepers are known to be who they are, but what they say is not necessarily to be trusted.†

Still, it's the only game in town, and short of asking viewers to send in "penny" postcards stating their preferences, it's the only way the television industry has of knowing how it is doing, although not, heaven knows, in terms of quality. Think of it. In all other forms of communication the public pays directly for what it gets; it pays for the right to read a newspaper, a magazine, a paperback, to go to the movies, to the theater, to a concert, or even (to stay with the public library analogy) to keep a book out overtime. Television viewers, cable aside, once they have paid the price of their set—and they will go to almost any lengths to find the cash for that—have all their home entertainment and, it is to be

---

†It has long puzzled me why in this computer age someone could not invent a way to combine the virtues of people (diary keepers) and meter ratings. Now, finally, in 1987 someone has. People Meters have been adopted by the networks to replace the Nielsen diary keepers, but have not at this writing filtered down to the local stations.

hoped, enlightenment for free. The one privilege they do not buy with the set, however, is the right to protest what they are receiving over the airways by withholding their patronage.

Newspaper readers dissatisfied with the paper's coverage of or slant on a story can stop buying the paper, and if enough people do so, it will adversely affect the paper's revenue. Television viewers have no such recourse. They can only make a conscious decision not to turn on their sets or deliberately to turn them off, and that, if Arbitron and Nielsen are on the job, may also take its toll on revenues, but by a far less immediate and convincing route.

One stricture that would protect the viewing public from a diet of too much mush would be if all stations, no matter who owns them or with whom they are affiliated, were compelled periodically to submit a detailed and *meaningful* application for renewal of their licenses instead of the entirely *pro forma* application the FCC requires. Such a strict demand does exist in England, where television is widely considered more sophisticated, and without it, according to Henry Becton, president and general manager of WGBH, Channel 2, such stellar series as *Brideshead Revisited* and *The Jewel in the Crown* might never have been made. These programs, seen in this country only on PBS stations, were produced not by the nonprofit BBC but by the commercial Granada Television, seeking "something that is a modest financial success but prestigious enough to keep their licenses, which have to be renewed every six years." Would that our FCC, which certainly speaks softly, carried such a big stick.

Such a system would be of positive benefit to Paul La Camera, who as vice-president/programming and public affairs is responsible for every hour in the broadcast day that is neither news nor network and is thus continually charged with weighing the quality of a given program against its probable ratings. It might be considered axiomatic that the higher the first goes, the lower the second is likely to be—axiomatic but fortunately not inevitable, and indeed by any reasonable standard Channel 5 programming under La Camera's guidance would easily qualify for renewal of a station's license if such mandatory arrangements existed in this country.

Still, La Camera, a tolerant man of good taste and an adventurous spirit, sometimes feels rather frustrated because, as he says, "The people around here tend to take what we offer for granted. What they should do is watch other television stations. They won't find a Cloris Leachman, who has won an Oscar and several Emmys, sitting in the next room reading a teleplay for a little local television station. Or ten video crews and a dozen still cameras fanned out all over the state working on a special we're going to call *One Day in the Life of Massachusetts*, or an investigative documentary we're doing on foster care in this state, to go with *No Safe Asylum*, the one we did last year on mental health. I honestly believe these are fine examples of a pretty good creative approach to programming."

But even though La Camera's predilections are understandably more directed toward *Chronicle* and specials, he is still in charge of the 4:00 to 6:00 P.M. weekday hours called Early Fringe that the station controls entirely with syndicated shows. "It's an important area for us as far as revenue goes," says La Camera. "You try to position your station in a certain direction against what the competition is doing. The independents, the UHFs, go after the kids, Channel 7 has four game shows stacked one after the other, but we're not in the game show business, so we try to stay with the dramatic form and situation comedies."

Maybe WCVB's offerings are better than game shows, but it seems to me that their 4:00 to 6:00 programming has been nothing to brag about. To be sure there have been all sorts of changes, swills, and dips in programming schedules, so staying abreast is sometimes like trying to keep track of quicksliver. But fundamentally such tired offerings as reruns of *Dynasty*, *The Waltons*, *Too Close for Comfort*, and the ubiquitous Archie Bunker in *All in the Family* have been the norm.

Considering that viewers are treated following the end of the *Midday News* to a steady diet of soap operas, it seems to me that a station as mindful of the public interest as Channel 5 might lighten the load between 4:00 and 6:00—or more properly put some heft into it—with programs that call for a slightly greater degree of awareness than the fare they have been offering.

There are those who will say I have been caviling about a time period when few serious people look at television anyway. Maybe so, but because these two hours are controlled by a station with a clearly manifested concern for excellence in local programming, I maintain they should be better.

And now, in the late summer of 1987, they finally give promise of being so. Thanks in large part to the good offices of Hearst, WCVB has snagged the popular, provocative Oprah Winfrey show away from the competition and will put it in the five o'clock slot, thus giving the station an infinitely better lead into the six o'clock news than they had with the long-over-the-hill *All in the Family*. Meanwhile, with the often arresting *Phil Donahue* moved to the four-to-five o'clock hour, the entire Early Fringe period is very much richer in content.

And, indeed, although the Hearst Corporation recognizes the importance of the previous owners' initiatives in news and special programs and will, according to John Conomikes, continue this effort, their thrust will be toward bringing in the best of first run network and syndicated shows. To this end CVB already has *Hill Street Blues* running at midnight and, in a major coup, has also signed up *The Bill Cosby Show*.

• • •

Here let me add a reminder about the difference between two kinds of local stations—independents and network affiliates. Independent stations have just that, an independence from the three networks, often because there *is* no network slot available in their particular market. This means they must fill all their hours with programs they generate themselves. Ideally this should mean less bondage from network domination and thus more freedom to do interesting, creative programming. In fact it usually means that those hours normally filled by affiliate stations with network programs are filled by the equivalent, which is to say syndicated shows that are about on a par with the 4:00-to-6:00 programs I have been complaining about on Channel 5. In some cities the dial location of independents is on the VHF band, which makes them more competitive with the network affiliates. In Boston, however, as in many other markets, the independent stations are on the UHF band, the high part of the dial where the signals are less powerful. What all this suggests is that an independent station is not necessarily as desirable as its name suggests.

"There's been a revolution in technology," Phil Balboni once pointed out to me, referring to his news department. "It has become so complicated that for a while it placed a huge demand on our engineering capability and on our reporters' way of doing their jobs. Because it was there, because we *had* the technology, we were expected to be live from anywhere in the country at any time. But fortunately we are past the worst of the wrestling now and should be able to take the technology more for granted and again put more emphasis on content."

Clark Booth, always a renegade, has this to say on that score: "We worry a lot about technical gimmickry. We try to stay competitive with a live presence from everywhere, but that's often a lot of folderol. Only a story that is truly breaking at the time of the broadcast is one which can be enhanced by a live presence, and that doesn't happen sometimes more than once a week, or even once a month. But it's regularly used because it's got that salty sort of immediacy—our man on the scene. Okay, great. But what does that add intellectually to the content of the story? Nothing. Much of the live presence is window dressing, pure and simple."

On the other hand, being live for a sports event is imperative, and it is in this context that TV shows off to its best advantage. We are seeing what is happening while it is happening at, say, a basketball or a baseball game or a tennis match, and we know those anonymous TV people have no control over the outcome. So a grand slam by the home team in the bottom of the ninth is very nearly as exciting on the small screen in our living room as at the ball park, especially as TV always does a good job of bringing us sights and sounds from the stands and dugout close-ups of high fives.

Fortunately the same generally favorable feeling carries over into the sports segment of newscasts, but the rule of thumb is that only 25 percent of an average local audience have a strong commitment to sports, 25 percent care nothing or feel negative if not downright antagonistic, and 50 percent just float, depending on whether anything on a particular day catches their fancy.

A projection into the regular news would probably reveal about the same interest level for each type of story. Twenty-five percent can't wait to hear the latest about a local police scandal, 25 percent are sick of it, and 50 percent are waiting with varying degrees of restlessness to be engaged.

It is for this half of his audience that Balboni and his lieutenants struggle constantly to improve, sharpen, hone, and, by experimentation, to change, reorder, add, subtract, and introduce new elements into their daily newscast mix.

They struggle because they know that the fortunes of their station depend heavily on their newscasts, which were once a loss leader but are now the largest revenue producer in the local broadcast day. They struggle because it is ego-gratifying, because they take the public interest seriously, because they know satisfaction with the product breeds complacency, and because they really do care.

I do not mean to suggest that Channel 5 is filled with nothing but self-righteous, breast-beating idealists. Certainly the station has its share of cynics, complainers, and frustrated artists, but by and large they are in the minority, and on the whole an upbeat atmosphere prevails.

Phil Balboni, it is true, is a tilter at windmills, but he is at the same time a pragmatic, realistic man; he has a concept of the near future shared by others in his profession which is compelling.

"I think there is now a great opportunity to do exciting work in a way we never even dreamed of five years ago," he says, and goes on startlingly to explain that what he is talking about is an opportunity for local news to become the "full-service electronic news source, actually supplanting national network news—supplanting and indeed *replacing* it with our own newscast."

It takes a moment to absorb this idea, but reflect on it and it begins to make sense, although first one must wonder how any one local station, no matter how potent, could conceivably cover a distant-breaking story—say, the Pan Am plane hijacking in Karachi—without having a reporter regularly assigned to cover Pakistan as the networks do.

Balboni explains: "What we are going to be seeing within the next few years is the development of a syndicated video news service—an AP, or UPI, that will be the complete analogue of the wire service machines that are in every newsroom, both electronic and print, in America.

"We will have a reporter presence everywhere, just as we

have now from the news services, only the correspondents will be carrying versatile, lightweight cameras so that when a story breaks we will have video sent by satellite and then Natalie Jacobson can say to our viewers, 'Today in Beirut such and such happened and here are the pictures of it.' "

Satellite technology, of course, is what makes this entire radical shift in television news coverage even possible to contemplate. And already in the satellite network Conus there exists a news-gathering service which permits WCVB and others in the six hundred or more stations in the Conus system to receive their stories directly, without any help at all from their networks.

Such independence is heady for local TV stations, making them ever stronger and better-positioned to take over the entire 6:00-to-7:30 evening news package. Says Fred Friendly, the highly respected television guru and keeper of the Edward R. Murrow flame, in *Broadcasting* magazine, "I think that gradually we will see the decline of the three networks. I think that major TV outlets is where most of the excitement and flexibility will be. Already the local stations are the ones with the huge blocks of time to offer serious TV journalists. . . . You will see some local station defections from the networks' evening newscasts within the next year simply because the networks don't offer the stations anything in those broadcasts that they can't already do themselves."

In the past year CBS, ABC, and to a lesser extent NBC have suffered serious financial reverses brought on by threats of takeovers, by excessive hiring, and by flattened advertising revenues. Furthermore, the growing strife between the news and entertainment divisions has meant that network evening news must often buckle under to entertainment demands by including in their scant twenty-two-minute shows at least one soft feature. (Recently, for example, I saw one which elaborated on a "unique pig race" in a Michigan county fair.)

Meanwhile, local evening newscasts with their hour of time have been more and more profitable, but still one part of the viewing public (especially the PBS aficionados) perceives local news to be focused only on rapes, murders, fires, and other dramas taking place within the home viewing area, with perhaps an obligatory nod toward some really big story taking place in the larger world outside. Emphatically these preconceptions are wrong. The thoughtful viewer will note that again and again, stories, especially lead stories on local and network news, are redundant. Corazon Aquino speaks to the Congress in Washington; all three Boston stations are there to cover it and lead with this story. Networks, predictably, lead with the same story and usually at no greater depth. In fact, as the authoritative communications magazine *Channels* points out, 70 percent of network news viewers are already familiar with the major stories before Dan Rather or Peter Jennings or Tom Brokaw reads them an hour later.

As a result, the *Columbia Journalism Review* notes: "There is no question that the center of gravity in television news innovation has shifted from the networks to the affiliates. But . . . one can't help wondering if local stations are ready for these new responsibilities."

Fred Friendly echoes this caveat, suggesting that this "radical change will require local stations to become more devoted to longer, more in-depth stories and more serious about their journalism in contrast to the networks headline service."

Such a challenge is grist for Phil Balboni's mill. "I cannot imagine letting these opportunities pass us by," he says. "If I didn't think it was going to happen, I don't think I could continue to work here. But it is going to happen. And when it does—I no longer say *if* but *when*—I would dearly love us to be the pioneer in this effort."

Asked what he realistically thinks of WCVB's chances to be in the vanguard of such a development, Balboni points

first to the obvious: "You can make more money doing this,"
he says. "If you add the additional time, that is, the network's
half-hour, you get to sell all the commercials. Naturally you
would have to increase your news budget to allow for this
extended time, but it's worth it in terms of the greater revenue you derive. And yet," he adds, "I often postulate this
new idea with a certain ambivalence because, although I
want to do it, I regret the loss of a very valuable news service
and of fine broadcasters like Peter Jennings."

He does, however, believe that many people from the
network will quickly be absorbed into local television stations, to the benefit of both. And in fact, just recently two
network figures have come to Boston to work: the already
mentioned Jay Schadler to Channel 5 and Dave Murray, the
Good Morning, America weatherman now at Channel 4.

So perhaps it *is* really beginning to happen. "The profit
is there, the capability is there, so all we need now is the
will to do it," says Balboni. "I'm sure that discussions about
this are being had in stations all over the country and that
somewhere, sometime, before too long one of them will
announce, in a nicely phrased press release, that they are
canceling the network news. And yes, certainly that could
be us. If you push hard enough, unless you're dealing with
people who are just very resistant, you'll ultimately prevail.

It should be noted that while Hearst is fully committed
to their Conus-satellite capability at WCVB—and more recently in their other stations—they are far from convinced
as yet that network news is doomed. "I think there'll always
be network news," says John Conomikes, while admitting
that this conviction is somewhat influenced by the fact that
all six Hearst stations are network affiliates (five ABC and
one CBS), thus strongly suggesting the desire to preserve
amicable relations.

• • •

Even as I wrote concluding thoughts, Rupert Murdoch reentered the Boston media scene—buying the small independent Channel 25—thus reminding me that for one mercifully brief period he actually owned WCVB, and causing me to wonder what would have happened if he had held on to it instead of spinning it off to Hearst.

Certainly the station, as we know it and have been talking about in these pages, would have ceased to exist. Who on the staff would have stayed on to become just another cog in Murdoch's brazen, soulless machine? Most probably not Phil Balboni or Paul La Camera or Jim Coppersmith or Martha Bradlee, Judy Stoia, Clark Booth, or married couples Natalie Jacobson and Chet Curtis, Debbie Sinay and Charlie Kravetz, Emily Rooney and Kirby Perkins, Linda Polach and Jim Boyd. Astounding, as I list only a few of their names, how many remarkable people there are in this one station.

Jim Coppersmith, while possibly not the most impartial observer, grows lyrical in describing his station's special qualities. "I can unequivocally state that this place is unique. There is rich soil here, tended by eccentric gardeners who care more about how beautiful their flowers are than how much they can get for them in the marketplace. This is a community of creative people who need to be stroked and allowed to spend a couple of extra bucks, waste a little here and there, to encourage them in their dreams."

And for the most part they have been encouraged. Why else would Channel 5 be the outstanding station it is? Why else such a heartening example of what can and should be done to make television come closer to fulfilling the role that was once envisaged for it as a strong positive force in our daily lives?

"The future of local television has never been brighter," says Phil Balboni. "Our horizons have never been higher."

If this coming of age is indeed to be a reality, Balboni had better be right. Probably the chance for at least some stations to put their own imprimatur on all the news that's fit to broadcast will come before the end of this decade. But to meet this challenge, those stations must immediately start gearing up, setting their sights on a far higher and more comprehensive goal than they have ever envisaged in their news programming.

To be sure, the networks will vigorously resist such a change; they will cling stubbornly to their often stated position that local news programs should be just that, disseminators of local news or at best of national news with a local angle. This is myopic. Television stations should serve their communities just as the metropolitan newspapers do. Obviously we do not relegate the *Boston Globe* or the *San Francisco Examiner* or the *St. Louis Post-Dispatch* merely to covering local stories while depending only on the *New York Times*, the *Wall Street Journal*, the *Christian Science Monitor*, and a few other so-called national newspapers to provide us with all the rest of the worldwide news.

"The genie is out of the bottle," say the true believers. And before long it will be up to the viewers to decide if they want to put it back in. Stations like WCVB Channel 5 and others of its kind all over the country must now grasp this opportunity to displace network news and exploit it fully to their viewers' advantage. If they succeed, as I believe they certainly can, they will be setting an exciting new standard for the entire television industry. And about time!

INDEX

ABC, 8, 51, 86, 93, 137, 202, 220; signs WCVB as affiliate, 42, 43, 111; on being preempted, 48

ACT (Action for Childrens Television), 45

AFTRA (Associated Federation Television and Radio Artists), 125

Albert, Dick, 71, 72, 117, 132, 139

All in the Family (Archie Bunker), 114, 115, 217

Allen, Peggy, producer *Good Day!*, 75–77, 79, 80–83, 86

Allen, Ron, 199

Amaral, Dick, 182, 189

Andres, William, 41

Anti-Defamation League of B'nai B'rith, 101n, 155

AP (Associated Press), 126, 220

Aqui, 197–198

Arbitron, 66, 67, 80–82, 185, 213, 214, 214n, 215

Arons-Barron, Marjorie, 195–196

Avruch, Frank, 193

Balboni, Philip S., 93, 104, 178, 184; calls meeting news staff, 11–13; efforts to acquire WCVB, 14–23, 27–30, 207; and chief correspondent, 102, 105, 106; and anchor teams, 118–119, 202–203; daily preparation for 6 P.M. news, 123–125, 128–129, 218–220; and *Chronicle*, 144–147; views toward Hearst, 209, 211, 222; on new technology, 218, 219; on future of local TV stations, 220–225

Balleni, Scott, 169, 170

Barker, Jim, 62

Barnicle, Mike, 155, 164, 165, 173

Baruch, Jordan, 41

Bates, Pat, 157

Baxters, The, 50, 51

BBI (Boston Broadcasters, Inc.), 6, 7, 15–17; struggle to win license, 31–39; board of, 39–41; affiliates with ABC, 42, 43; staff morale at, 49–50; early programs, 45–47, 74; financial success, 50, 52; sells station to Metromedia, 52–54; launches *Chronicle*, 144–145; fosters unity of purpose, 207; mentioned, 115, 118, 196, 199

Becton, Henry, 215

Bennack, Frank, 15, 16, 28, 56, 209, 211

Bennett, Robert: as president Metromedia, 6, 7, 11, 17, 53–55; meets with executives seeking to buy WCVB, 18–21; role in sale to Hearst, 23–30; negotiates ABC affiliation, 42, 43; past experience in TV, 44; on preemptions, 47, 48; on staff morale, 49, 50; staff farewell to, 55, 56; and *Chronicle*, 145, 147; innovates Metromedia Playhouse, 172; audacious hiring practices, 178, 199, 200; and editorials, 196; guest at Hearst party, 208; mentioned, 100, 105, 119, 210

Beranek, Leo, 48, 115, 118; leads fight to acquire Channel 5, 35–37, 39–41; hires top newscasters, 43, 44; on BBI's sale of station, 52–54

Berger, Joshua, 139

Bill Cosby Show, 203, 217

Booth, Clark, career of, 182–184; as writer-reporter of *A Time Remembered*, 185–189; on technical gimmickry, 218–219; mentioned, 224

Boston Globe, 16, 32, 34, 66, 94, 103, 107, 155, 166

Boston Herald Traveller, 6, 15, 16, 48; fights to retain Channel 5, 31–34, 36–39

Boston Marathon, 131, 161–166

Boston Pops, 208

Boston University, 115, 174; School of Communication, 178, 179

Boyd, Jim, as anchor of *Eyeopener*, 61–67, 72–73; and *Midday News*, 87–89; and Challenger disaster, 93, 94; mentioned, 224

Bradford, Krista, 203

Bradlee, Benjamin, Jr., 103, 104

Bradlee, Greta, 107, 108

Bradlee, Martha, as chief correspondent, 102–109, 124, 133, 140; auditioned by CBS, 107; mentioned, 100, 224

Brawer, Jeff, 168

Bringola, Tom, 19, 20, 29

Broadcasting, 219

Brokaw, Tom, 220

Brown, Matthew, 40, 41

Buehl, Dave, 59, 63, 64

Burch, Dean, 37, 38

Burke, Susan, as anchor of *Eyeopener*, 57, 61–65, 72; and *Midday News*, 89, 93

Cable News Network (CNN), 58, 88, 91, 93

California, University of, 126

Candlepin Bowling, 190–192

Capital Cities, 8

Carnegie Commission Report, 168, 169

Carney, Karen, 169

CBS, 8, 42, 184, 220; auditions Martha Bradlee, 107; offers job to Natalie Jacobson, 118; Challenger disaster, 90–95

Chromakey screen, 59, 70n, 99

Chronicle, 143–166; origins of, 143–149; as successful magazine show, 150–161; demographics of, 159–160; on the air with Boston Marathon, 161–166; mentioned, 81, 82, 112, 114, 115, 116, 178, 179, 193

Churchill, Winston, quoted, 186, 187

City Line, 197–199

Clancy, Harold, 34, 36–38

Close, Glenn, 78, 79

Collins, John, 194

Colson, Charles, 37

Columbia Journalism Review, 221

Conomikes, John, 209–211, 217, 223

CONUS (Continental United States), 93, 129, 219

Copeland, Bob, 62, 69–71

Coppersmith, S. James: as general manager, WCVB, 13, 16, 146; efforts to acquire station, 14, 20–22, 29; farewell to Bennett, 56; and Debbie Sinay, 110, 111; attitude

toward *Chronicle*, 114, 147, 149; reads editorials, 196; on weekend news anchors, 202, 203; views toward Hearst, 210, 211; on WCVB staff, 224; mentioned, 197, 207, 224
Correia, Manny, 169, 170
Cottle, Tom, 78, 79
Court of Appeals, U.S., 34, 38
Curtis, Chet, 44, 51; and sale by Metromedia, 5–15 *passim*; as anchor 6 P.M. news, 117–119, 133, 139–142, 203; early career, 119; response to rumor, 203; mentioned, 81, 224

David, Nathan, 36–38
Deland, F. Stanton, 41
Dickinson, Richard, and graphic design, 96–101
Dickson, Harry Ellis, 208
Donahue, Phil, 76, 77, 84, 111, 112, 217
Dowling, Mike, 131
Dukakis, Michael, 208
DVE (Digital Visual Effects), 98, 100
Dynasty, 111, 114, 217

Eastern Airlines, 124, 134
Edwards, Jack, 130, 131
Elizabeth, Queen of England, 51, 119
Ellis, Tom, 118, 119
Emmys, 97, 104, 105, 168, 216
ENG (Electronic News Gatherer), 59, 63, 65
ESS (Electronic Still Storer), 64, 79, 88, 99
Eyeopener, The, 57–73, 86, 88; mentioned, 118, 125

Fasciano, Bill, 168, 170
FCC (Federal Communications Commission), 6, 30, 32; and the Channel 5 case, 31–38; designates prime access time, 143; failure to maintain broadcast standards, 205, 215; mentioned, 44, 52
Fernandez, Mike, 131
Ferraro, Geraldine, 80
Five on Five, 194, 195
Folsom, Dave, 136–138

Fonda, Henry, 55
Fortas, Abe, 38, 39
Fratangelo, Dawn, 203
Friendly, Fred, 184, 219, 221, 222

Gabriel Award, 197
Gardner, Robert, 41
Geballe, Bob, 151–153, 160
George, Laurie, 162, 163, 165
Gillis, Don, 43, 191–193
Gollobin, Ron, 65
Good Day!, 44, 50, 74–86, 193, 195, 199
Good Morning America, 88, 89, 223
Goodwin, Doris Kearns, 194, 195
Gould, Stella, 166
Great Entertainment, The, 193
Greater Boston Civil Rights Coalition, 101n
Greenberg, Jeff, 95
Guillen, Dr. Michael, 94

Hall, Andria, 150, 150n; as producer of *Chronicle*, 151–153, 156–158, 161–166; as on-air reporter, 151, 152, 155, 156; as anchor, 151, 154, 154n
Handlin, Oscar, 41, 44, 49, 50, 196
Harper, Jack, 124, 129, 130, 140, 201, 203
Harvard University, 124, 132, 135
Hasty Pudding Club, 123, 127, 135, 136, 141
Hearst Corporation: acquires WCVB, 5, 7, 11–15, 22, 23, 28, 55, 56; favorable auguries, 207–208; questions posed to, 209, 210; response by top executives to, 210, 211; on future of network news, 223; mentioned, 173, 224
Henning, John, 44
Heston, Joseph, 75, 77, 82, 195, 200
Hill Street Blues, 217
Hoffman, Andy, 159
Holmes, Karen, 199
Holton, Gerald, 41
House Call, 17, 45, 50
House on Salem Street, The, 178–182

HUT (Houses Using Television), 66, 67

Hynes, Jack, 43

IBEW (International Brotherhood of Electrical Workers), 63, 125

Ithaca College, 119

Jabberwocky, 45, 50

Jacobson, Natalie, 51, 61; and sale by Metromedia, 5–15 *passim*; as anchor of 6 P.M. news, 117, 118, 121, 122, 128, 133, 142, 203; turns down CBS offer, 118; early career, 119–121; as narrator of *Somerville High*, 168, 170, 171; and *The House on Salem Street*, 180–182, 180n; mentioned, 81, 154n, 221, 224

Jennings, Peter, 93, 220, 222, 223

Jeopardy, 210

Johnson, Dr. Timothy, 17–19, 45, 167

Johnson, Nick, 38

Jones, Hubie, 194

Jordan Marsh, 115

KABC-TV, 81–82

Kane, Mary Ann, 93, 94, 124, 129, 135, 141

Kater-Arruda case, 124, 129, 130, 140

Katz American Television, 110

Kennedy, Edward M., 208

Kennedy, John F., 32

Keohane, Derm, 72

Kerry, John, 208

Kidder, Peabody, 14, 20, 29

Kirschenbaum, Jerry, 160, 166; early career of, 176–178; as writer-producer of *The House on Salem Street*, 178–182

Kluge, John: as owner of Metromedia, 14, 17–19; meets with WCVB executives, 20–23; sells Metromedia to Murdoch, 24, 25; commitment to Hearst, 25–28; buys WCVB, 53, 54; guest at Hearst party, 208

Knowles, John H., 41, 45

Koppel, Ted, 155, 208

Kraemer, Chuck, 90, 135, 141

Kravetz, Charles, 115, 168, 184; prepares for 6 P.M. news, 123, 124, 135; as producer of *Chronicle*, 145, 147, 148; mentioned, 224

KRON-TV, 128

KTTV-TV, 44

Kukiewicz, *see* Curtis, Chet

Kuttner, Bob, 94

La Camera, Paul: efforts to acquire station, 13, 14, 17–21, 207; and sweep months, 81; and station finances, 111; and *Chronicle*, 145–148, 150, 160; as mentor, 197; views toward Hearst, 208; on creative approach to programming, 215, 216; mentioned, 75, 224

Langhart, Janet, 79, 82, 84

Latson-Gitten, Donna, 197

Laughinghouse, Isaac, 63, 64, 72, 86

Law, Bernard Cardinal, 98

Lawless, David, 164

Leachman, Cloris, 173, 216

Lear, Norman, 51

Levy, Phil, 62, 63, 73; producer of *Midday News*, 86, 88, 89, 94

Lewis, Rose, 58, 59, 62, 63

Lowell, Jim, 62, 63, 72

Loy, Myrna, 55

Lynch, Mike, 117, 130–132

Lyons, Paula, 90, 135, 141

MacNeil-Lehrer, 206

Made in Japan, 135

Massachusetts Correction Institution (MCI) Framingham, 156–157

Masso, Joe, 198

McAuliffe, Christa, 90, 94

McKenna, Kathy, 153, 162

McNerney, Shirley, 90, 93, 94, 124, 135, 141

Mehegan, Peter, as anchor of *Chronicle*, 150, 154, 160, 161–166; as moderator of *Five on Five*, 194

Metromedia: sells WCVB, 5–7, 10, 23–27; staff reactions to changes in ownership, 15, 17, 18, 146; contributions to WCVB, 53–55; Playhouse, 172–173; mentioned, 14, 102, 207

Midday News, 86–95, 196, 216; reporting Challenger disaster, 90–95
Miller, Arthur, and *Miller's Court*, 44, 199–201
Mills, Mark, and *Chronicle*, 153, 154, 158–161, 163
Minot, Linda, 157, 158
Minow, Newton, 32, 33, 114
Mirabella, Lori, 169, 170
Morita, Pat, 173
Mostone, Crescenzio, 179–181
Mostone, Liberdati (Albert), 181
Murdoch, Rupert, buys six Metromedia stations, 5, 7, 10, 11, 15; acquires UHF station in Boston, 223; mentioned, 16, 173
Murray, Dave, 222
Murrow, Edward R., 184

NBC, 42, 220
Needham, Massachusetts, 6, 35, 137
Nelson, Avi, 194
New Hampshire, University of, 120
New York Times, 10
NewsStar 5, 138
Nielsen, 66, 67, 80–82, 185, 213n, 214, 215
Nixon, Richard M., 34, 37
Nurse, Karl, 199

O'Callahan, Jake, 189
Our Town Revisited, 112

Paintbox, 98
Patriots, New England, 91, 98
PBS, 206, 207, 214, 220; *see also* WGBH-TV, Channel 2
Peabody, George Foster, award, 51, 168
Peabody, Skip, 64
Perkins, Kirby, 124–127; at Hasty Pudding Club, 135, 136, 138, 139–141; mentioned, 224
Perlman, Itzak, 208
Polach, Linda, 9, 224; as producer of 6 P.M. news, 123, 125, 126, 128–130, 132, 133, 135, 142
Pourvu, William, 41, 50, 199
Prose, Eileen, 75, 79, 82
Public service campaigns: *World of*

Difference, 101, 155, 197; *Don't Be Pushed*, 197

Quantel, 100
Quinlan, Sterling Red, 32n

Rather, Dan, 220
Ratings, importance of, 65–67, 80–82, 115, 122, 123, 202–204, 212; ways of measuring, 213, 214, *see also* Arbitron, Nielsen
Record American, 34
Rhode Island School of Design, 97, 100
Richardson, Mary, as anchor of *Chronicle*, 150, 154, 154n, 160, 164–166; and *Main Streets and Back Roads*, 166
Rodgers, Bill, 164
Rodriguez-Howard, Myra, 198
Rooney, Emily, 91, 93, 104, 184, 224; prepares for 6 P.M. news, 123–126
Ropeik, David, 91, 124, 128, 141
Roycroft, Alan, 169, 171
Ruben, William, 213
Rubin, Phil, 191
Rule, Elton, 42–43

Salatich, *see* Jacobson, Natalie
Schadler, Jay, 202, 203, 222
Schmid, Lisa, career of, 167, 168; as producer of *Somerville High*, 168–171; as producer of dramas, 172–174
Sharfman, Herbert, 33, 34
Shawmut Banks, 101n, 155, 156
Shirer, William L., 189
Sinay, Deborah, as general sales manager, 109–116; mentioned, 224
Sloane, Susan, and *Chronicle*, 153, 159, 160, 164
Smith, Jim, 125, 129
Somerville High, 168–172
Sorebella, Robert, 170
Special programs, early: *Jabberwocky*, 45, 50; *Medical Call*, 45; *House Call*, 45, 50; *To Live in New England*, 46; *So Frail a Thing*, 46; *Symphony*, 46; *No Fish Tomorrow*, 46; *How Safe Is Logan Airport*, 46;

Busing: A Tale of Two Cities, 46;
*The Frightening Feeling You Are
Going to Die*, 47; *The Baxters*, 50,
51; Later programs: *Summer Solstice*, 55; *Our Town Revisited*, 112,
113; *Straight Talk: Gays in Boston*,
113, 197; *Growing Pains*, 172;
Blind Alleys, 173; *Secrets*, 167,
173, 209; *A Special Peace*, 173; *Somerville High*, 168–171; *The House
on Salem Street*, 178–182; *A Time
Remembered*, 185–189; *One Day in
the Life of Massachusetts*, 216; *No
Safe Asylum*, 216
Stallings, Caroline, 62, 70
Stallone, Sylvester (Rambo), 124–127,
135, 136, 139–141
Stoia, Judith, as managing editor of
Chronicle, 145, 147, 148, 160, 161;
co-author *Somerville High*, 168;
and specials, 173, 182; mentioned,
206, 207, 224
Sunday Best, 193
Supreme Court, U.S., 34, 38, 39
Sweep months, 80–82

Thistle, Jim, 104, 145, 146
Time Remembered, A, commemorates
World War II, 185–189
Too Close for Comfort, 114, 217
Turner, Ted, 8
Twentieth Century–Fox, 5

UPI (United Press International),
125, 219
U.S. Embassy, Lisbon, 133, 140
Utah, University of, 103

Wall Street Journal, 10, 213
Walters, Barbara, 208
Waltons, The, 217
Ward, Don, 39
Washington Post, 103
WBZ-TV, Channel 4, 35, 50, 135;
People Are Talking, 77, 80, 85; rat-
ings race with WCVB, 122, 123,
202; *Evening Magazine*, 145, 146,
149, 159; mentioned, 88, 120, 178,
183
WCVB-TV, Channel 5: sold by Metro-
media, 5–14; efforts by executives

to acquire, 16–23; positions of Bennett in sale, 23–30; BBI wins license to operate, 31–39; first signal
on air, 39; affiliates with ABC, 42,
43; early programs on, 45–48, 74,
75; syndicated shows pay off, 50,
51; financial success of, 52; BBI
sells to Metromedia, 53, 54; Metromedia contribution to, 54, 55,
173; farewell to Bennett, 55, 56;
Eyeopener, The, 57–73, 196; de-
scription of newsroom, 61; reporting the weather, 68–72; *Good
Day!*, 74–86; and sweep months,
80–82; *Midday News*, 86–95, 196;
reporting Challenger disaster, 90–
95; graphic arts at, 96–101; role of
chief correspondent, 102–109; role
of general sales manager, 109–116;
daily preparation for 6 P.M. news,
123–134; signal transmitted to and
from, 136, 137; 6 P.M. news aired,
139–142; creates program for prime
access spot, 143–148; *Chronicle* as
successful magazine show, 150–161;
typical *Chronicle* offering, 161–166;
shows preempting prime time,
168–171; 178–182; 185–189; dearth
of weekend programming on, 190–
191; *Candlepin Bowling*, 190–192;
Five on Five, 194, 195; editorials
on, 196; and community relations,
196–199; *Miller's Court*, 199–201;
change of weekend news anchors,
201–204; as an exemplar, 207;
views toward Hearst, 207–211; programming under La Camera, 215–
217; sports on, 219; future role of
local newscasts, 220–225, Coppersmith on staff of, 224
WGBH-TV, Channel 2, 51n, 178,
206, 207, 215
WHDH-TV, Channel 5, 6, 42, 45,
119; fights to keep license, 31–34;
goes off the air, 39, 43
Wheel of Fortune, 115, 210
Wilder, Thornton, 112
Winfrey, Oprah, 217
Wishner, Mimi, 125
WLVI-TV, Channel 56, 120
WNEV-TV, Channel 7, 42, 43, 50;

Morning Live, 77; attempts to lure WCVB staff to, 105, 119, 135; *Entertainment Tonight*, 149, 159; mentioned, 88, 178, 202
WNEW-TV (New York), 21, 23, 44
World of Difference, A, 101, 155
World War II, 186–189

Wornick, Susan, 72, 87
WTTG-TV (Washington), 44

Yee, Leetha, 58, 62–64, 73

Zebra, 138, 139
Zucker, Warren, 99